INFINITE POSSIBILITIES OF SOCIAL DREAMING

INFINITE POSSIBILITIES OF SOCIAL DREAMING

W. Gordon Lawrence

KARNAC

First published in 2007 by
Karnac Books Ltd.
118 Finchley Road
London NW3 5HT

British Library Cataloguing in Publication Data

A C.I.P for this book is available from the British Library

ISBN-13: 978–1–85575–493–5

Edited, designed, and produced by
Florence Production Ltd, Stoodleigh, Devon
www.florenceproduction.co.uk

www.karnacbooks.com

Printed in Great Britain by Biddles Ltd, King's Lynn, Norfolk

For Dame Ruth Silver, DBE, who has taken Social Dreaming into the management of education institutions and the making of new lives.

The known is finite, the unknown infinite; intellectually we stand on an islet in the midst of and illimitable ocean of inexplicability. Our business in every generation is to reclaim a little more land.

[T.H. Huxley, 1887.]

Ultimate reality can be thought of as a vast reservoir of infinite possibilities of thoughts awaiting a thinker, from the derivatives of which, the transformations, we cull from time to time elements that seem to belong together, that form a pattern or constant conjunction. These elements we bind together by a name or a number so that they become available to be filled with meaning, so that we come to understand the emotional significance for us of this particulary bit of reality. This understanding can then join up with another constant conjunction to accrue further meaning and so on indefinitely.

[Joan and Neville Symington, (1996), *The Clinical Thinking of Wilfred Bion*, p. 123, London: Routledge.]

CONTENTS

ACKNOWLEDGEMENTS

This, the fourth book on Social Dreaming, would not have been possible without the effort of the authors of the chapters. To them and the many people they have collaborated with in Social Dreaming Matrices in diverse countries. I am immensely grateful. They have gone against the opinion of the majority to see the potential of Social Dreaming for the times we in which we live. I want to acknowledge the intellectual bravery of Presidents of the International Society for the Psycho-analytic Study of Organizations who have made the conditions for Social Dreaming to be a feature of the annual conference.

The preparation of this book was greatly aided by Shivani Patel who retyped the manuscript after it had been copy-edited by Ellen Emerson, and to Ashish Patel who did wonders with the final typescript after Joan Hutten tidied up the inevitable mistakes. Finally, to Bipin Patel who has quietly subsidised Social Dreaming Ltd. for so many years,

I owe an enormous debt.

CONTRIBUTORS

VERRED AMITZI trained in psychology and sociology and now works as an Organizational Consultant with Go-on in Israel. She undertakes a substantial amount of adult education. She publishes frequently. She does Social Dreaming (SD) regularly with both Palestinians and Israelis as well as group relations training.

ALASTAIR BAIN *B.Sc. (Econ.) Hons (London), M.A. (Chicago), FAISA* is a socio-analyst, founder member and a director of the Centre for Socio-Analysis in Melborne, Australia. Social Dreaming, and its use within organizations as Organizational Dreaming, forms a major part of his working life through its use on a weekly basis with close colleagues at the Centre, as a tool of cultural enquiry, currently into "Citizenship", and "Transitions" (Point Lonsdale Conference), exploring "Gender and Authority" as in the recent Hyderabad Workshop sponsored by Chindu (a Dalit organization), explorations of the building of Communities through "Mallacoota Dreaming" Conferences, in training programmes, action research, organizational consultancy, and group relations conferences.

His publications on Social Dreaming include "Social Dreaming and Organizations: The Potential" (1994), "Not Two and Not One" (2003), "Organizational Dreaming" (2006), and the article in this book "The Organization Containing and Being Contained by Dreams: The Organization as a Container for Dreams (1)". Most are available at www.acsa.net.au. Email: A.G.K.Bain@gmail.com

HANNI BIRAN is a clinical psychologist, a psychoanalyst and a group analyst. She is lecturer on group psychotherapy at the Tel Aviv University School of Medicine and also at Haifa University programme of psychotherapy. She is a member of the Tel Aviv Institute of Contemporary Psychoanalysis and a member of the Israeli Institute of Group Analysis.

JOHN CLARE is a psychotherapist with a background in art, sociology and psychoanalysis. Formerly a lecturer in Sociology at the University of London, he is a founding member of the Multilingual Psychotherapy Centre. He is an expressionist painter with recent shows in London and Wales. His involvement with Social Dreaming developed by working with W. Gordon Lawrence, and for three years he was the host of the IMAGO Social Dreaming Matrix. He has written a number of papers and chapters, including "Predicting the Future—Social Dreaming and Catastrophe", "Samuel Beckett and Psychoanalysis" and "Multiple Psychotherapy—the loss of mother tongue". He currently works in private practice as a psychoanalytic psychotherapist in London.

DONATELLA ORTONA FERRARIO is Italian by birth and family upbringing, educated in the United States and bilingual. She has worked as a journalist, mainly with the American Press and TV in Rome for over thirty years (AP, NYT, CBS News) as well as promoter of the arts and mediator between different cultures as a press officer.

Following a demanding experience as volunteer and coordinator with an association for HIV+ children and their families (Arhche), she followed a course in Gestalt Counselling. She became attracted to Social Dreaming when collaborating with W. Gordon Lawrence during his first introduction of SD to the University of Rome in 2001. Her journalistic background highlighted the socio-political context of dreams, while the Gestalt training and volunteer work enhanced the disposition to multiversity and empathy which are necessary in the kind of relatedness of a SDM.

Since then she has participated in monthly SD Ongoing Matrices and has conducted SDMs in institutions such as hospitals, volunteer organizations and the University of Rome (La Sapienza) and the University of L'Aquila.

FRANCA FUBINI is a psychotherapist, group analyst and organizational consultant who lived and trained in the United Kingdom, India, and Italy where her practice is based. She has taught Management of Human Resources at Perugia University. She is the co-founder in the integration of the arts in the psychotherapy of psychosis and was involved in the creation of "Blossoming in Europe", a programme that links Europe in the exchange of cultural events.

Alongwith Dr. Lilia Baglioni she founded in Rome an institute for Social Dreaming in Italy.

HERBERT HAHN is currently a Senior Visiting Fellow in the Centre for Psycho-Social Studies at the University of the West of England. He works as a Psychoanalytic Psychotherapist and Organizational Consultant having previously been a Chartered Clinical and Occupational Psychologist. Trained in Tavistock-Leicester and Bath-Tavistock Group Relations, and Dyadic and Group Analytic work he is a member of the Group Analytic Society, the British Association of Psychotherapists and the British Association for Psychoanalytic and Psychodynamic Supervision. He is accredited as a Training Therapist and Supervisor by the Severnside Institute for Psychotherapy, Bath Counselling and Psychotherapy Courses.

He has served on the staff of the Tavistock Clinic, the Tavistock Institute of Human Relations, European School of Management Studies, Cassel Hospital and taught in the Psychology Department of the Universities of Bristol and Witwatersrand. His consultancy work includes senior management selection, mentoring team building and career development programmes.

He has had a passionate engagement with W. Gordon Lawrence's SDM for the past fifteen years and has hosted and co-hosted SDMs in the UK, Europe and South Africa. He has published numerous articles in professional journals, contributed chapters to books, and co-edited with Anna Chesner *Creative Advances in Group Work* (2003, London: Jessica Kingsley).

DR W. GORDON LAWRENCE is a MA (Aberd.), Dr rer oec (Bergische) is a managing partner of Social Dreaming Ltd, London. He is a visiting professor at the University of Northumberland, Newcastle, the New Bulgarian University, Sofia, and at La Sapienza, the University of Rome. Formerly, he held a visiting professorship at Cranfield University, Bedford. He is on the editorial board of *Free Associations* (UK), *Freie Assoziation* (Germany) and *Organizational and Social Dynamics* (UK). He is a Fellow of the Australian Institute of

Socio-Analysis and a Distinguished Member of the International Society for the Psychoanalytic Study of Organizations. He was on the scientific staff of the Tavistock Institute of Human Relations (1971–82). discovering Social Dreaming before he resigned, consultant at Shell International (1982–85), and President of the International Foundation of Social Innovation (1985–90). Since then he has worked independently. He publishes regularly.

THOMAS A. MICHAEL is Professor Emeritus at Rowan University in New Jersey, Principal and Senior Consultant at the Dialogue Centre for Counselling and Consulting. He taught organizational development, organizational behaviour, and business policy in the College of Business at Rowan for over twenty-five years. He was founder and administrator of the Master of Administration Programme at Antioch University in Philadelphia. He is an ordained Presbyterian minister, having served two congregations in New York State and is on the national staff of the Presbyterian Church in USA in personnel referral and career counselling. He is a member of the International Society for the Psychoanalytic Study of Organizations. The Colloquium on Violence and Religion, the A.K. Rice Institute, the Philadelphia Centre for Organizational Dynamics. He has consulted, conducted workshops, and published in the field of organizational development and Social Dreaming.

HELEN MORGAN is a Senior Member of the British Association of Psychotherapists and is a training analyst and supervisor for the Jungian Analytic Section of the BAP. She works mainly in private practice as an analyst and also supervises in both the individual and the group setting. Her background is in therapeutic communities with adolescents and in adult mental health. Her publications include a number of papers on Social Dreaming Matrices convened at IAAP Congress in Zurich 1995, Florence 1998, Cambridge 2001 and Barcelona 2004 as well as in other settings. Other papers include the following: "Between Fear and Blindness—the white therapist and the black patient", *BAP Journal*, January 1998, "Modern Western Society – the making of myth and meaning" in *Jungian Thought and the Modern World*, Ed: E. Christopher & H. Solomon, FAB, 2000. "The New Physics through a Jungian Perspective" in *Jungian Thought and the Modern World* Ed: E. Christopher & H. Solomon, FAB, 2000, "Exploring Racism", *Journal of Analytical Psychology*, Vol. 47, No. 4, October 2002.

DR BURKARD SIEVERS is Professor of Organizational Development in the Department of Economics, Management and Social Sciences at Bergische Universität Wuppertal in Germany, where he teaches and writes on management and organization theory from a psychoanalytic perspective and an action research approach. He received his Dr. Soz. Wiss. from the University of Bielefeld in 1972 and has held visiting appointments at various universities abroad. Dr. Sievers is co-editor *of Freie Assoziation—Zeitschrift für das Unbewusste in Organization und Kultur*. He was awarded the 1995 International Award for Participation from the HBK-Spaarbank in Antwerp (Belgium) for his book *Work, Death, and Life Itself. Essays on Management and Organization*, Berlin: de Gruyter 1994. He has directed various Group Relations Conferences and led workshops on Social Dreaming, Organizational Role Analysis and Social Photo-Matrix. He is President of the International Society for the Psychoanalytic Study of Organizations for the period 2005–2007 and co-director of "Organizations in Depth", an International Professional Development Program held in Coesfeld/Cologne, Germany. Most recent publication: Newton, John, Susan Long & Burkard Sievers (eds.) (2006): *Coaching-in-Depth: The Organizational Role Analysis Approach*. London: Karnac.

PETER TATHAM is a medically qualified doctor who retrained at the C.G. Jung Institute in Zurich. Since returning to England in 1979 he has had an analytic practice outside London. He has lectured in England and abroad on Jungian subjects and also conducted Social Dreaming Matrices in various places and situations. His book *The Making of Maleness* was published in 1992, and he continues to research and lecture on new attitudes to male archetypes and fathering. He recently published a chapter in *Creative Approaches to Group Work*, edited by A. Chesner and H. Hahn (2001).

ALI ZARBAFI is a UKCP Analytic Psychotherapist and Trainer working in the NHS and private practice. He was a founder member of the Imago Mult-lingual Psychotherapy Centre. He is interested in the multi-lingual and refugee/immigration experience and runs workshops entitled "The Refugee Experience" for mental health professionals. He has been involved in Social Dreaming for many years and has used it in his work with organizations.

Introduction

The chapters in this book indicate the endless possibilities of free association and amplification in Social Dreaming. Although each writer has conveyed this, there still exist in their texts more detailed connotations and possible meanings of particular dreams. In a sense, their chapters are only beginnings for the reader to expand, as none, is in any sense a complete, final version of the potential meanings of dreams in a particular Social Dreaming Matrix.

The first chapter is an exploration of the infinite possibilities of Social Dreaming for using the social unconscious of the culture, as opposed to the narcissistic preoccupations of the individual unconscious. This highlighting of the shadow side of life, paradoxically, illumines consciousness with all its rational thinking. The social unconscious opens new vistas for the mind and endless possibilities of understanding.

Burkard Sievers, in Chapter Two, leads off with a description of Social Dreaming work with Social Democrats in Austria. While in our private dreaming we are dealing with the existential challenges of our lives, when we are dreaming in the Social Dreaming Matrix our horizon expands to include the neglected parts of our public life. Sievers addresses these issues as they surfaced in the Matrix.

The theme of politics, which runs through all the chapters, is discussed by the practitioners of Social Dreaming in various countries: Germany, Israel, and South Africa, and with refugees in Italy.

Hanna Biran, in Chapter Three, describes Social Dreaming with Palestinians and Israelis. The Matrices were organized in the context of an exhibition of paintings by Wolf Werdigier in Jerusalem, Tel Aviv, and Ramallah. The paradox is that both Israelis and Palestinians dream the same anxiety dreams, which are harrowing for mothers. The dreams illustrate what people project on to their society, and show the psychic power of the social unconscious with its political consequences.

Verred Amitzi takes a much broader view of Social Dreaming by situating it in the history of Israel from 1988 to 2004. The dreams provide an unconscious commentary of daily life in Israel, set against the complexity of living in a country beset by intense struggles of nationhood.

In Chapter Five, Herbert Hahn takes us to South Africa where he has done Social Dreaming for a number of years. He shows how in the post-apartheid struggles people make the move from adversarial politics to active engagement in building a new society by surfacing (in their dreaming) previously unspoken hopes and fears.

Donatella Ortona, Eleonara Planera and Laura Selvaggi take us to Italy in Chapter Six. They describe Social Dreaming with a group of female political refugees (from Rwanda, Eritrea, Nigeria, and Albania) seeking asylum in Italy. They demonstrate that Social Dreaming can be done with ordinary people who have had tragic, extraordinary experiences. They suggest that dreaming may be (is) the *natural* way the mind, having registered traumatic experiences, repairs the body-mind of an individual, so that it is restored to a balance of living in the changing environment.

Continuing in Italy, Marinelli and Girelli explore the icons of the social dream with groups of students at the University of L'Aquila. In Chapter Seven they eruditely discuss the place of the oneiric icon in Social Dreaming against the background of a university in transition describing the reactions of students in different faculties.

Helen Morgan describes in Chapter Eight, a Social Dreaming Matrix with the British Association of Psychotherapists. She makes the point that dreams tell us what reality *is* and not what we think it ought to be. Using the Matrix as a container for the divisions in the BAP between Freudian and Jungian thinking, she concludes that participants in a Social Dreaming Matrix make themselves available for thought which allows for the emergence of images, associations, symbols, and ideas, but not of conclusions, thus emphasising the multiverse nature of Social Dreaming.

Peter Tatham has cooperated with Helen Morgan on Social Dreaming at the annual conferences of the International Association for Analytical Psychology. They hold a Matrix each day and Tatham describes the Matrix with over a hundred people in Zurich, Florence, and Cambridge.

Both Chapters Eight and Nine describe dreaming work with "professionals" in contrast to the other chapters which are all with "non-professional" people.

Thomas Michael has done pioneering work in Social Dreaming with churches in America, reported in *Social Dreaming @ Work* and *Experiences in Social Dreaming*. In Chapter Ten, he presents a case study of a consultancy in a public assistance organization in a mid-Atlantic state in the US. Through the Social Dreaming Matrix the participants were able to identify the boundary issues of their department, which led them to address the work issues of their organization. He demonstrates the usefulness of Social Dreaming in organizational consultancy.

In Chapter Eleven, Ali Zarbafi, John Clare, and I have written about Social Dreaming at the Hay-on-Wye festival in England sponsored by the *Guardian* newspaper. This was a remarkably rich Matrix composed of people in their role as writers or embryonic writers. We focus on the idea of creativity and Social Dreaming. Predictably, because of the imaginative nature of the participants, the dreams are exciting and "riveting". We have now done it for two years.

Alastair Bain addresses the problem of the "container" for Social Dreaming. Using Australian organizations as his example, he argues for the idea of Organizational Dreaming, pointing out how it differs from Social Dreaming. To be sure, he is right. But in discovering Social Dreaming, I have debated with myself for years what it should have been called. I thought about Social Systems Dreaming and various other names. In the end I went for Social Dreaming because this included other configurations, like organization, and still made it applicable to particular social groupings.

The next two chapters, Thirteen and Fourteen, offer the initial thinking on and experiences of the Dream Reflection Group (DRG) and the Creative Role Synthesis (CRS), which Bipin Patel and I have devised. Both arose from Social Dreaming. The former makes possible a considered exploration of the dreaming and the themes of the Matrix to produce a synthesis of the findings.

The CRS comes out of the experiences of Social Dreaming and is a way whereby the individual can address the existential puzzle, or paradoxical challenge, or impasse, that they may be experiencing as they discharge their various roles in life.

Chapter Fifteen illustrates CRS. Franca Fubini presents case studies of how it can work. This is entitled, "The Sphinx looks at the Individual".

These last three chapters are to underline the practical developments of Social Dreaming. From the beginning the Social Dreaming Matrix was conceived of as being of the world. The Social Dreaming Matrix is always part of a programme lasting a few days at the minimum. Various events have been tried in the past, and we outline here the most recent ways we have tried to set Social Dreaming in the culture of the society as a tool of enquiry.

CHAPTER ONE

Infinite possibilities of Social Dreaming

W. Gordon Lawrence

Social Dreaming

Social Dreaming was discovered in the early 1980s at the Tavistock Institute in London. Its focus is on the dream and not the dreamer. It is done with a set of people who come together to share their dreams. This goes against the accepted belief, even dogma, that the study of dreaming can only be pursued in a one-to-one relationship, where one of the participants is a trained psychoanalyst.

Social Dreaming devised a method whereby dreaming could be pursued by a set of people working together. This collection of people was termed a Matrix. The Social Dreaming Matrix mirrors, while awake and conscious, the "matrix of the undifferentiated unconscious" (Ehrenzweig 1967) which operates during sleep. Since dreams arise from the unconscious, the hypothesis was that the configuration, or setting, to receive dreams had to render unconscious thinking salient. The idea of "group", which was an obvious choice, was rejected. If "group" had been chosen, the conscious, inter-personal relationships of the dreamers would, inevitably, have become more important and interfered with the dreaming process. The idea was that dreams were to be the currency of the configuration, not the relationships, nor the feelings about the authority (transference) of the people dreaming. As it is, transference issues are to the dreams, not to any individual.

By focusing on the dream and not the dreamer, not only does the Matrix provide a safe mental space for the participants—who never have to defend their dreams or themselves—but it also approaches dreaming from a novel perspective. This perspective is from the thinking embedded and carried in the dream, which arises from the culture of the participants' environment; all the systems within which the dreamer interacts and relates, such as a company organization or a community. The personality of the dreamer is not the concern of Social Dreaming. The dream becomes a shared object of the Matrix; once dreamt by an individual, it can be regarded and added to creatively by all the participants.

Social Dreaming makes possible the examination of the social unconscious, which comes into existence when three or more people relate through their individual unconscious. Through their unconsciousness they discover an added quality to their unconscious mind which would be beyond the capabilities of their individual unconscious. This is the social unconscious.

The Social Dreaming Matrix created a mental space at a conscious level which provided a container for the social unconscious to be addressed through dreaming and free association. The discovery of this new container for receiving and working with dreams resulted in a change in the contained. The form, contents and metaphors of dreaming changed. No longer was the dream dreamt for the benefit of one person and her task of discovering her innermost world, but was now for the many, for those in systems, organizations and institutions. The focus was not on the individual but on individuals in their culture. Social Dreaming freed the dream from being gagged and bound by the world of "I" and allowed it to speak of and address the social world of humanity.

By focusing on the thoughts and knowledge within the dream, a whole new view of dreaming is being developed. Through the use of free association a thought contained in a dream is expanded. Again, through amplification, the thoughts in the dream are related to the culture of the society; a thought may spark off a reference to a film, or any cultural artefact, that is part of the dreamers' repertoire of what is consciously not known.

Through this thinking process, the thoughts contained in the dreams start to undergo a process of transformation. This capitalizes on the fact that the thinking processes which we use while awake are totally different from those used while sleeping. This is the difference between conscious and unconscious thinking.

While we are awake and conscious, we are dealing with perceptual input, mathematical symbols, signs, and words, which we relate logically. By contrast, while we are dreaming we think in imagery, which we relate by means of figurative language. In the in-between state, when we are in reverie and day-dreaming, we use fewer words and signs and are less logical but note the resonances of similarities and metaphor.

The sequencing of ideas while awake follows strict logical categories; while asleep and dreaming, these categories interrelate in ways that we could not imagine while awake. This is because the unconscious is non-logical and fuses everything and every experience into a one-ness.

While we are conscious, we are highly self-reflective, making use of the "I", or the ego, to think through our experiences; but in dreaming we are not "egocentric" for the "I" is less important as we lose ourselves in the "thereness" of the dream.

Whereas conscious logic is concerned with discrimination and classification, because the mind is making propositions to itself about one thing and another and how they are related, the unconscious does not recognise such differences. This means that novel relationships can be discerned.

The boundaries around "knowledge system" are thick and well-defined while we are awake and conscious, but as we dream these boundaries are loosened; occasionally they become thin and disappear. Consequently, our thinking is within these structured subsystems while awake, but less within and more across subsystems of knowledge while asleep (Hartmann, 2000, p. 67).

The unconscious is based on infinite sets which have no ending and no boundaries, but the conscious mind is structured with finite sets of the relationship between two things, or ideas, related to the person as thinker. These triads are the basis for our logical, rational thinking (Matte-Blanco, 1975).

Social Dreaming recognizes and works with these differences in thinking and pays attention to the unconscious, celebrating the matrix of the undifferentiated social unconscious because the Matrix is a source of human creativity and inventiveness. This spectrum of thinking is not to be seen in either or terms but in a both and sense for each is dependent on the other to sustain the holistic mind of humanity.

Dreaming and evolution

Dreaming has been part of our mental lives from the time that our forebears developed the pre-frontal areas of their brains and the visual areas of their cortex. Before that, in the early stages of evolution when our beginnings were as one-cell animals, millions of years ago, we engaged in a form of proto-dreaming as the cell interacted with its environment and began to rehearse and test how it would relate to its eco-niche. This took millions of years.

Dreaming has fascinated humans from the time they first learned to speak of this bizarre, strange, imaginary realm they entered while asleep. This imaginary realm was the basis for the creation of tools and artefacts that make up civilization as we know it. They came into being as humans experienced the social world they inhabited and used their imagination, fantasy and dreaming to create them. Humans created their culture as a product of the projections of their dream world onto the actual lived world they experienced. The possession of this imaginative realm gave humanity its genius.

Evolution and projection

Human beings' cultural projections can be of two kinds; the benign and the destructive. There are all the cultural artefacts, like tools, buildings, literature, and all the arts that make for a constructive life. The less benign, more destructive, aspect of dreaming is that it can fuel the projections mankind makes on its surrounding world and affect political strategies for governing people. Hitler and all other dictators are a case in point. Imagination, fantasy and dreaming are intertwined mental processes, each sustained symbiotically by the other. Hitler was able to project his fantasy of a united Germany and Austria with disastrous results. Aided by propaganda and political circumstances in which Germany suffered punitive reparations, unemployment, and inflation, Hitler was able to persuade others to accept his grandiose fantasy of a Germany that would be strong and feared, lasting longer than any previous civilization. He persuaded the majority of the population that he was right in his thinking.

Any dissent of the minority was kept in check through a mixture of half-truths, deceit and dread of persecution. Those who disagreed were persecuted. Hitler projected his fantasy, which became more and more accepted as people took it into their inner, private world, by introjecting his public ideas. Hitler and his followers' powers of persuasion were unique. The Third Reich became an in-grouping which relied on the creation of an out-grouping, defined by Hitler as enemies of the Reich: it included anybody foreign such as people of the conquered vassal states, Jews, gypsies, homosexuals, the handicapped, and non-believers of the accepted correctness of the Nazis. To be sure, his imagination and fantasy were flawed and distorted, but they had started from his dreaming mind, although no record of his dreams exists.

The situation was complex. Because of economic conditions in Germany which resulted in unemployment and inflation, Germans were driven psychically into social anxiety because they felt themselves victims of the occupying military forces imposed by the Treaty of Versailles. There was little hope in large sections of the population who felt persecuted by the prevailing social, economic and political conditions. Thus there arose a wish for a messiah who could explain why those conditions existed, to deliver them from their travails by offering certainty, security and a better future. Hitler's ideas were presented in simplistic, easily understood terms.

His programme at first was only articulated by a small minority, while in the majority there was an unconscious brooding on his ideas in dream and fantasy. While not all would have thought of the draconian measures of Hitler, gradually many persuaded themselves they were acceptable. The majority of the population empathised with Hitler's political fantasy because their unconscious wishes resonated with Hitler's simplistic policy. A symbiotic relationship built up between Hitler, the "projector", and the majority of the population, the "introjectees". One could not exist without the other; otherwise the "projector" would have become an insane, shunned individual.

A unity of unconscious thinking from the imaginary realm swamped the minds of the majority of the population. There was little difference between the fantasy of Hitler and the fantasy of the German population. Today, as we watch documentary films of the times, we are amazed at the enthusiasm of the crowds for their Führer.

This example of the Third Reich and of mutual unconscious projection illustrates the uncomfortable, but incontrovertible, fact that we are inclined to forget that all cultures and civilizations are products of the human mind. As Frankl writes,

> We tend to consider social behaviour to be conditioned by external circumstances and regard ourselves as victims of "objective reality". But any study of man's social reality, the external conditions as well as our responses to them, must acknowledge that it is humanity which creates its conditions and, what is more, does so largely unconsciously and then depends on the conditions it has created (Frankl, 1989, p. xvii).

The study of dreaming

The accepted explanation of dreaming for early humankind was that it came from the gods. It was a message from the transcendent, "other", world. How else could the phenomenon be explained?

Freud, with his startling *The Interpretation of Dreams* (1900), overthrew such explanations with his pursuit of scientific rigour. The problem was that Freud was a product of his times. The science of his times was posited on cause-and-effect which was the organizing metaphor of mechanistic science. The world was seen as a gigantic machine of the stars and planets with the result that human kind's behaviour was conceptualised on the same underlying principle.

Nevertheless, Freud founded psychoanalysis and led the way in interpreting dreams. He regarded dreams as the expression of wish-fulfilment on the part of the patient. Freud and his followers focused on the individual and produced a great deal of important psychological data. But, in their pursuit of understanding the individual psyche, they tended to focus less on the social dimensions of dreaming. The cultural aspects of dreaming were disregarded, except by some psychoanalytically-orientated anthropologists such as Roheim (1934, 1982).

Jung, who broke from Freud, developed a far wider notion of psychology. He believed that order exists in the human psyche, but not always in a cause-and-effect relationship. Jung was fascinated by the new sciences which were emerging in the early twentieth century. He postulated that there could be "meaningful coincidence", in time which originated in the psyche, independent of time and space. This notion of acausality explains chance, or randomness, which is the simultaneous relatedness between phenomena and events that are causally unconnected. Not every relationship between events, phenomena and experiences can be explained in cause-and-effect terms. In conjunction with Wolfgang Pauli, a natural scientist, Jung went on to identify the acausal "orderedness" of science. This particularly applies to dreaming.

Social Dreaming accepts synchronicity. In a Social Dreaming Matrix, where the dreams come from infinite sets of the unconscious, it is possible to work out connections and links between the dreams which are not apparently causally related. One hypothesis, for example, is that the very first dream of a Matrix is a fractal of all the dreams that are to follow. Free associations give this fractal more substance.

Dreaming as a tool of cultural enquiry

Social Dreaming engages the cultural aspects of dreaming. Human beings have the capacity to think what they like. There is no obvious limit on what can be thought, using fantasy and the imagination. The thoughts may not be remarkable; they may not be useful; but they are always novel. New experiences, new contexts, and new interactions create a continuous spectrum of different impressions and pictures of the world.

This, John Barrow believes, indicates that there are limitless possibilities for what we can think. Barrow calculates the

> ... number of neural configurations that the human brain can accommodate. He estimated that it can represent about $10^{70,000,000.000,000}$ possible "thoughts"—for comparison there are only about 10^{80} atoms in the entire visible universe. The brain is rather small, it contains only about 10^{27} atoms, but the feeling of limitless thinking that we possess derives not from this number alone but from the vastness of the numbers of possible connections that can exist between groups of atoms. This is what we mean by complexity, and it is the complexity of our minds that gives rise to the feeling that we are at the centre of unbounded immensities. We should not be surprised. Were our

> minds significantly simpler, then we would be too simple to know it (Barrow, 2005, p. 19).

Dreams are formed in the matrix of the unconscious as images, but in the act of recounting a dream in ordinary discourse each person has to translate the original images of the dream into words, or pictures and paintings, to render the raw images in communicable terms.

It can be argued that every recounted dream is an emerging truth because the veracity of the undifferentiated imagery of the dream eludes the speaker. How can the imagery be recaptured? In the process of free association, particularly with a large number of listeners to a particular dream in a Social Dreaming Matrix, one can attempt to reveal the "truth" of the dream. But it will always be an approximation of what the absolute truth might be, which is why working hypotheses are so critical in Social Dreaming. By the use of the working hypothesis we avoid *hubris*, the sense of omnipotence and omniscience of the classical interpretation, and we open up collective exploration in order to have a more scientific mode of addressing reality which, as human beings, we are always trying to understand, but know we are never able to capture.

The gap between the image and its description is a form of engagement, i.e. a creative act involving both feeling and thinking. This work of promoting understanding has shape and is continuous in the Matrix.

Social Dreaming is a humbling experience. But that challenge opens new possibilities. The challenge is that in attaining the limits of comprehension the human mind discovers the new thinking which is embedded in the unknown.

Social Dreaming deals with dreams, which are a product of the unconscious and the infinite, i.e. the unknown. Therefore it takes us out of the comfort zone of empirical, rational thinking and inducts us into the knowledge and understanding that can only be attained through experience, introducing us to acausal explanations and synchronicity.

Social Dreaming could not have been discovered without the ground swell of new scientific thinking that took place in the twentieth century. The rational purity of thought, enshrined as an ideal by the Enlightenment philosophers, was put into question by the discovery of the unconscious by Freud. This was made manifest by writers like Joyce and Burroughs. These writers saw that the ambition of linguistic purity was just an illusion. Burroughs famously cut up rational sentences and pasted them back together to make apparently irrational ones, giving new meanings to words in a new context.

Burroughs and Joyce were anticipating the communication revolution that has hit us since the PC and the Internet came into existence. Joyce wrote in Finnegans Wake that

> . . . every person, place and thing in the chaosmos of Alle anyway connected with the gobblydumped turkery was moving and changing every part of the time; the travelling inkhorn (possibly pot), the hare and turtle, pen and paper, the continually more and less intermisunderstanding minds of the anticollaborators, the as time went on as it will variously inflected, differently pronounced, otherwise spelled, changeably meaning vocable scriptsigns (Ed. Joyce, 1992 p. 118).

Psychologically, Joyce was anticipating the Internet revolution. In that conceptual leap, he was going against the linear thinking of his times. There are two characteristics of the World Wide Web and human thought which are in opposition to the traditional linearity of the written text. "They are the simultaneity and multiplicity of supplied information at a single moment in time. Also, there is the additional value given over to the visual image as an information transmitter." (Julian Manley, 2005, personal communication.)

This elaboration of experiences pressing more and more meaning out of them, leads to a more enriched culture and exploration of the human condition. This cultural exploration was aided in the twentieth century by the modernist movement for "the retrieval of experience or interiority" (Taylor, 1989, p. 461).

This "pursuit of interiority" has been a force at work particularly in the cultural life of the West, to counteract the instrumentality of industrialization.

> Twentieth century art [modernist] has gone more inward, has tended to explore, even to celebrate subjectivity; it has explored new recesses of feeling, entered the stream of consciousness,

> spawned schools of art rightly called "expressionist". But at the same time, at its greatest it has often involved a decentring of the subject: an art emphatically not conceived as self-expression, an art displacing the centre of interest onto language, or onto a poetic transmutation of itself, or even dissolving the self as usually conceived in favour of some new constellation (Taylor, 1989, p. 546).

As far as dreaming is concerned, psychoanalysis, of whatever school, follows the path of the former, i.e. the celebration of subjectivity. Social Dreaming, on the other hand, is involved in a transmutation of the dream to find a "new constellation" of the meanings of the dreams made available to the Matrix, because it is more centred on the flow of experience expressed in the dream and on the novel forms of the unity of these experiences. Although these two paths seem contradictory, paradoxically they go together. The exploration of the first can model the exploration of the second, and vice versa.

Concretizing the idea of Matrix, it can be likened to a weaving built from the loom of minds. The Native American dream-catcher is an analogy. But, of course, the Matrix only exists in the mind. Because in the Social Dreaming Matrix the status of the dreamer is irrelevant, there is equality between the voicing of the dream and related associations. There are no constraints on thinking—everything is possible.

The unconscious and the infinite

It is hypothesized that Social Dreaming inducts participants into infinite possibilities. The infinite is just one thing after another. There can be infinite regression or infinite expansion; either an endless subdivision of numbers, or a limitless addition of numbers.

The unconscious and the infinite are linked. The tentative working hypothesis is that the individual unconscious is an infinite regression of personal vestiges of memory, based on individually-registered images of experiences with emotions. It is like two mirrors facing each other where the images going on forever, diminish in size in infinite regression. The more these are examined microscopically, say in psychoanalysis, the more these vestiges of memory become clear and expand in significance and meaning.

Bollas has written about the "unthought known" (Bollas, 1987). Each of us carries in the recesses of our inner world traces of memories of experience, which are never thought about and are, therefore, out of consciousness. However, in later life we can have an experience which will trigger the unconscious, vestigial memory bank. Once this happens, we think about it. Once thought, it becomes known to us. This articulation of the "unthought known" makes a difference to us individually, no matter how seemingly insignificant it may be.

So, crudely, it can be hypothesized that the individual unconscious is infinite regression of bounded psychic experiences, images, and emotions, but the social unconscious is boundless expansion, or progression, of cultural experiences, images, and emotions. Theoretically, both have the potential to be known. (These are not absolute, clear-cut definitions, and infinite is being used in the poetic sense rather than the scientific.)

When three or more persons are together, the chances are that their unconscious minds will resonate; the unconscious images will echo one another because the unconscious web of emotions is unconstrained by the demands of relationship. Thus, the social unconscious comes into existence. Through both the individual and social unconscious, which is a mixture of progression and regression of images, the infinite begins to be discerned, but only occasionally.

Both the individual and the social unconscious have finite limits. They each, ultimately, can be known. The boundaries of the individual and social unconscious are not clear-cut but are always merging with the infinite. The way of accessing the infinite is to pursue the finite in all its dimensions and directions. This is done in Social Dreaming by exploring the social unconscious. As the social unconscious is explored in the Matrix there follows an infinite expansion of its images.

Because Social Dreaming started from an intuition in the late 1970s, the first forays were tentative. People were attracted to it because it was a form of entertainment or art. As it developed, working hypotheses were formulated: some fell by the wayside because they were found wanting in their explanation of the evidence. Scientific explanations are essential for Social Dreaming to become accepted by both participants and hosts of the Matrix.

It is postulated between the individual unconscious and the pursuit of epiphany by the individual subjectively exploring the experiences of the psyche, to enter the stream of consciousness. There is also a parallel between the infinite and the social unconscious, in relation to the anti-subjective movement for the retrieval of experience of the natural world and its cultural artefacts. This leads to new ways of apprehending the features of the world which go beyond the straightforward descriptions that served humanity so well in the past. This is a cultural epiphany. By entering the flow of experience of the world, new ways of describing the world had to be discovered. Eliot, Joyce, Burroughs, and Derrida were among the pioneers.

This is analogous to the discovery that everything that exists is structured on a hidden world of waves and particles, and that these particles look as if they are acausally connected. The juxtaposition in poetry or art of images, words, metaphors, and similes reveals new apperceptions of that which had been explained in straightforward ways before. This resulted in epiphanies of a cultural order in contradistinction to the subjectivity of the personal.

Social Dreaming works with the dream as made available to the Matrix. The content of the dream is elaborated through free association and amplification. By concentrating on the flow of experience of the dream, delving deeper into the cultural experiences it symbolizes, and not on the subjectivity of the dreamer, a new domain of cultural significance is laid bare, which is based on the "multiverse" of meanings that a Social Dreaming Matrix engenders. By mobilizing the social unconscious and the infinite in the Social Dreaming Matrix, infinite connections can lead to the transformation of thinking. The Social Dreaming Matrix has the potential for realizing infinite possibilities.

But we live in a world governed by the "instrumental" frame of mind. The unconscious is a counterforce to this rational, logical thinking. The experience of a Social Dreaming Matrix provides a thinking space for the social unconscious to be rescued and valued. The "instrumentality" of our daily lives cannot be replaced by an unconsciously-governed, "affective" frame of mind, and it would be undesirable that it be so. What can be opened is a dialectic conversation, a more studied social dialogue, between the unconscious mind and the instrumentality of the world of consciousness. Thus, human beings can nourish the roots of their creativity to reveal the true nature of their social, political, and economic world with all its specious, temporary successes in the context of the everlasting tragic aspects of the human condition.

To conclude: Emily Dickinson opens an untitled poem, written probably about 1862, with the line "I dwell in Possibility" (Franklin, 1998). John Broadbent (2000, personal communication) writes that this line probably refers not only to her inveterate use of metaphor but also may refer to living and thinking. In a real sense, the experience of a Social Dreaming Matrix invites any participant to "dwell in possibility" of their dreaming. The possibilities arise from the unconscious, both individual and social; by experiencing these, one can contemplate the infinite.

CHAPTER TWO

Social Dreaming with social democrats in Austria

Burkard Sievers

This is a description of a Social Dreaming Matrix held with a group of Austrian Social Democrats in 1999, who were local council members in one of the federal states. The idea of holding the Matrix came up at a workshop on Organizational Role Analysis (cf. Krantz & Maltz, 1997; Lawrence, 2006; Newton, Long & Sievers 2006; Sievers & Beumer 2006), that I had organized in Vienna. One of the participants approached me during the coffee break to ask whether I knew someone who could do a workshop with him and some of his colleagues on the presence of "the occult" in social democratic factions of local councils in the federal state of Austria, where he lived.

Even though I was quite astonished, indeed nonplussed, about what might be meant by "the occult", I got into a conversation with him. It soon became obvious that what he had in mind—even though he did not quite use that "terminology"—was to address the unconscious aspects of the politics of the local council's factions. He was concerned that it had proven again and again that even the best results of meetings and retreats remained only on paper and could not be put into action unless personal and structural "blocking mechanisms from the occult" were taken into regard. When I told him about Social Dreaming, he soon took it as an appropriate and fascinating frame for our collaboration.

Some time later we arranged a four-day workshop with the title "The Other Side of the Organization". He and seven of his colleagues took part. As its focus was the special situation of these local councils, I had a hunch that a mere attitude of "without memory and desire" would not be sufficient to do justice to this special request and the kind of work we were up to. I therefore asked him for some literature and documents to help me to get a better understanding of the history of Social Democracy in Austria. Even though there would certainly be parallels to the situation and history in Germany, I wanted to be familiar with their specific context.

The Social democratic Workers movement appeared to have had a major impact on the social and political development of Austria. Social Democrats claim to be *the* important freedom movement in this country.

> In the first phase of activities it [i.e. the Social Democratic Workers movement] has fought to establish political democracy and the republic, in the second it has built up the welfare state, and the task for the third phase is to develop political democracy and the welfare state into more of a social democracy. (Sozialistische Partei Österreichs, 1978, 3)

In comparing the 1998 party programme (SPÖ-Bundesgeschäftstelle, 1998) with that of 1978 (Sozialisitische Partei Österreichs, 1978), I was surprised to learn that the party had not only changed its name from *Socialist Party of Austria* to *Social Democratic Party of Austria,* but it had also given up most of its original rhetoric and language—and—one could assume—part of its original mission. Whereas in 1978 it was stated: "we *socialists* are *fighting* for man's freedom and dignity . . . against all suppression and exploitation through political despotism and private economic or state-capitalist power" (Sozialisitische Partei Österreichs, 1978, 1; my emphasis), the 1998 document emphasizes that *Social Democrats*

> are *obliged* to honor the ideal of a humane, democratic, and just society. . . . This ideal of a humane society is the aim whose realization we gradually hope to accomplish by democratic competition with other political concepts (SPÖ-Bundesgeschäftstelle, 1998, 3; italics added).

The transition from a party for the workers to one "for all working people" (ibid., 4) is consistent with the fact that even though for more than a century actually the *socialists* had been "the leading power of societal change in Austria" (Sozialistische Partei Österreichs 1978, 45) it is now—in 1998—the *Social Democrats* who are taking credit for having achieved the great progress of previous years. By 1998 what had been called "capitalism" in 1978 had been updated to "inconsiderate neo-liberalism and unsocial neo-conservatism".

From the documents I received in advance, it was obvious that the local councils played a significant official role in the Austrian governmental system. Based on a tradition of more than a century, municipalities and local councils are democratically elected institutions with a high degree of autonomy. In addition to their governmental and administrative tasks, they provide the majority of services required for the daily life and safety of citizens living in municipalities, for example kindergartens and schools, water supply and waste disposal, police and fire brigade. With the exception of a few towns and cities, almost half of these municipalities have no more than 2,500 inhabitants (cf. Neuhofer n. d.; Brünner, 2003). Though one might assume that the policies of the local councils would reflect those of the national parties, that is actually not the case. In fact it seems that national political principals were less influential at the local level and in rural communes, in particular, than on the level of the federal states and the republic. I thus imagined that the members of the local factions that I would be working with might feel a certain estrangement from their comrades in the state and republic parliaments. Evidence elicited during the workshop supported this presumption.

The relevance of this issue for our upcoming work with dreams became truly clear when—during the first night of our workshop—I had the following dream:

> *In a conversation with a colleague I am becoming aware that she/he is an illegitimate child of Adolf Hitler. When I expressed my astonishment—because it was not known that Hitler had either illegitimate children or intensive relationships with women—the colleague showed me a list of names of women*

> *with whom Hitler had intimate relations, which had been published in a book.* I had arrived as a German in Austria and had decided not to share this dream in the next Matrix—not least because it is the role of the host to a Social Dreaming Matrix to provide sufficient space for the dreams of the participants—but it soon became obvious in the further course of the workshop that my dream reflected a theme present in the participants' dreams. Subsequent to the workshop—when I was writing an earlier version of this paper (Sievers 2001)—I learned from Der Spiegel that five "of the six women to whom Hitler had felt close during his life" had either tried or succeeded to commit suicide (Meyer & Wiegrefe, 2000, p. 141).

Even though the participants were somehow hesitant and sceptical about working with their dreams and associations during the very first Matrix—an experience which is not uncommon for a first session—they soon became fascinated with the insights they were able to glean from their dreams on ignored and neglected parts of their own political reality. In the second dream shared in the first Matrix, *one participant had been at a political event, which included a winning ceremony of a lottery. The first prize had been an inflatable car.* The associations related to this dream were largely concerned with the question of whether the results of their political work and election campaigns were ultimately only hot air in a gigantic balloon. Unlike actual lotteries in Austria, the first prize was not even a real car.

The SPÖ's (Social Democratic Party of Austria) low chances of winning an upcoming election had certainly created an air of disappointment and resignation in these participants. The wretched plight of social democracy came up again and again in the dreams and associations during the workshop.

In the next participant's dream, the leader of this group is quite certain that he does not have to remember his dream because there will be minutes. Only when he wakes up does he realize that no minutes had been taken. Associating to his own dream, he wonders *if, due to the common practice of taking minutes of meetings, the dream of socialism has been lost.*

"We stay permanently onstage but have forgotten the text" is the association of another participant. *Would it not be much more appropriate to stick a needle to the balloon* (the first-prize car) *or pull out the stopper to let the air out?* Party events (such as those in the current election campaign) are experienced as overblown and mere cabaret. One of the participants questioned what they represent on the stage. *Scene shifters, lighting technicians—we are no leading lights, we don't play a role,* was the response.

One of the next dreams is referred to by the dreamer as the "Storm and Stress Dream" (Sturm und Drang Traum). It consists of episodes from the 1968 student revolt. *That was a situation in which one was playing a role. The masses of slaves* (i.e. students) *were competing with the professors. We staged disruptions at the Burgtheater and the Opera* (in Vienna). *We arranged happenings and lustily gave speeches with lots of joy.*

The second dream shared by the same participant takes place in the institute where he is employed. *The director has introduced a procedure by which all events are to be evaluated. He presents and vehemently defends this quality control procedure, for which he is made responsible, at a board meeting—despite the fact that he himself cannot identify with it. My heart is not in this work, but it has to be done. It is not my dearest wish to accomplish this task.* Another participant comments that there is not too much difference between the dream and reality.

In one of the following dreams there is a reference to a house named "Chapel", which is owned by the SPÖ. It is associated with Charlie Chaplin's film *Der große Diktator*—"The Great Dictator"—in which Hitler stands on a box to appear taller than he actually is, while Mussolini sits on a couch. *Today we do not live a full life. The generation of our fathers participated in the war with enthusiasm. That was tragic, but they have been betrayed. Who is betraying us today—or are we betraying ourselves?*

To what extent these questions about the future of social democracy are both subliminal and, at the same time, paralysing for the everyday life of these participants and connected to the party's current identity crisis becomes evident in the following associations during the first Matrix: *If what we have accomplished with social democracy at present actually is a dream, then we have to fight against this dream. That is a gigantic story. When we or the generation before us still had a vision that was worth fighting for ... Today it is only a matter of winning elections!*

The Matrix on the following morning began with a dream in which *one of the participants attends an event with the SPÖ chairman and president of the federal state in which the workshop took place. Amongst other issues, the political leader spoke about a strategy for the world's future. He had made a very bad impression and ended up enraged.* To everyone's surprise, the dreamer—who had had no previous knowledge of such an event—had just read in that morning's newspaper (after he had had his dream) that this had really happened the previous night. The fact that he, somehow in synchronicity with the newspaper editors, had dreamed a situation that actually had happened without him knowing about it, left the rest of us in a state of stupefaction and wonder. It also made us realize what aspects of everyday reality the work with dreams could reach if one is prepared to allow for it.

The associations raised by this dream again referred to the discrepancy between the party's public "persona" and the actual reality and reinforced the contrast between the previous revolutionary commitment and the current shallowness, falseness, routine, and betrayal. *The situation is almost like in Kafka; one has instructions that ultimately remain unfulfilled.*

As before, the generation of fathers comes up in the associations. *While our fathers' generation wanted to change the world—in the war our goal was just to defeat our fathers in the 60s and 70s. As a matter of fact we should fight against our corrupt party, a system that exists. I have lost the dream, the vision of what social democracy embodies. There is nothing more worth fighting for. What is important has already been accomplished; we don't have to fight for it.*

The fact that the meeting of the European Social Democratic Party leaders (Blair, Klima, Schröder etc.) took place in Vienna the very weekend of the workshop contributed to the disillusionment concerning the present situation and found its expression in the dreams. The newspapers referred to the meeting in Vienna as a family reunion. This was reflected in associations to how the social democratic body of thoughts could be transferred into the next generation. *What do we have to offer our children? Despite the ongoing and increasing globalisation we have abandoned the internationalisation of socialism in our party programme!*

This particular association apparently refers to the fact that the phrases "international solidarity of all people as the strongest weapon in the fight against suppression and injustice" and "the pledge to the principals of the socialist international" were omitted from the 1998 edition of the party programme.

After bread and wine had been distributed among party members or potential voters in two other dreams, the question was raised: *What has happened to all the good wine of socialism. Has it turned to water? Is the reason that nobody wants it any more the fact that it has turned sour and does not taste good any more?*

The ideological shift in the way the party sees itself—as expressed in the two party programmes—reflects the fact that most of the original socialistic dream had been realized in the last decades and there was not much left worth fighting for. As "social democratically co-determined policy had not only helped increase the level of welfare but also overcome traditional fetters of thinking and action" (SPÖ-Bundesgeschäftstelle, 1998, 4), faith in this dream and its revolutionary creative potential may have faded. Election campaigns have degenerated into a competition between political parties, who compromise for the mere sake of gaining a majority.

Although a sense of betrayal seems to be inherent in several of the dreams and associations—the illegitimate children of Hitler, the inflatable car, the scene shifters and lighting technicians, the new evaluation procedure, the good wine of socialism, the brain surgery—I wonder what it means that the actual experience of betrayal could not explicitly be addressed in either the Matrix or the Mutual Consultation Group. In trying to understand this, another, much earlier experience of a Social Dreaming Matrix in Germany comes to mind. In a Matrix in which we were working both in English and German neither the participants nor we as hosts were able to relate to the word *Buche* (beech tree) and its meaning. We were working in a Protestant house named after Martin Niemöller. In the garden in front of our working room was a sculpture of him symbolizing the seven years he spent in the concentration camps *Sachsenhausen* and *Dachau*. The word *Buche* apparently was too close to *Buchenwald* (beech forest), another concentration camp, in order for it to be associated to (cf. Lawrence, 1998, 24f.).

As expressed in one of the associations to the "Chapel" dream, the memory of the fathers who had been betrayed in the Second

World War led to the question of whether the members of the Matrix were either being betrayed by the Social Democratic Party or were, in fact, betraying themselves. The betrayal was related to the fantasy that the accomplishments of the Social Democratic Party had made the dream a reality. That led to the thought that, if so, this "dream" had to be fought against and destroyed in order to revitalize the original one. If such a betrayal was part of the political reality, they were not only the victims but were also playing an active role—quite similar to the protagonist in the dream about the new quality control procedure *despite the fact that he cannot identify himself with it*. In retrospect, I think the politically propagated belief that the old dream had been fulfilled was not only an illusion but a lie that "desecrated" the original dream of socialism. Recognizing this would have created an unbearable despair in the group. To acknowledge this despair and ultimately to uncover the betrayal would have required a "revolutionary potential" other than the one expressed in the dream of the student revolt in the late 60s.

Whereas resignation and a feeling of hopelessness dominated the dreams and association during the first days, the dreams of the last Matrix showed unimaginable and unexpected possibilities for the future of social democracy. Perhaps the effort required to achieve these possibilities would actually be worth it. As demonstrated by the following dream in particular, this was not primarily a matter of strategies or programmes but related to the symbolic nature of transformations and metaphors for how change could take place.

Images of telephones and cell phones had already appeared in previous dreams shared in the Matrix. One dreamer introduced his dream in the following way: *In a dream many unrealistic things come up which appear in the dream as normal and logical. On occasions like this I like to continue dreaming and am really glad about it*. And he continued: *Someone has sent me a case by fax that contains a small box. In the box was a meal of meat and goulash sauce. As the meal was not accessible through the fax, I could not eat it. Then an amazing technical solution occurred to me. I converted the fax into e-mail. Suddenly the meal was edible. It tasted good. The happy ending is due to the transformation, which came to my mind. I am quite proud of myself.*

In the dialogues during this workshop I shared some thoughts on the organizational shadow (Bowles, 1991) and on the "psychotic organization" (Lawrence & Armstrong, 1998; Sievers, 1999). These ideas resonated in the following dream fragment and the associations towards the end of the workshop: *My wife and I were in a place where we stayed over night. The house was much too big for us; we were five people. At breakfast we were four at the table. My cell phone rang. Our son was calling me from the second floor and told me that I should come up; he wanted to show me something. He had a device similar to a cell phone, a transmitter. One had just to press a button in order to talk with someone without a cell phone.*

The conversation refers to an acquaintance of mine whom I had not seen for years. She is a heavy drinker; she is drinking far too much. She had to undergo surgery; one of her kidneys had to be removed—a surgery which usually is not that severe. But instead her brain was cut open. One could see that half of the head was empty. She cannot remember the other half. The brain is supposed to be . . . can be perceived as a highly developed control centre, which processes a lot of information. But here it was half empty, the electrical impulses were somehow organized.

The associations to this dream concerned the potential meaning of the other half of the brain. Does the amputation of the brain or one part of the brain not stand for the way we are accustomed to cope with psychosis, with the psychotic parts? By questioning the method of Social Dreaming, are we not repeating the way in which we previously dealt with mental disease and psychosis? Psychotics have been treated in earlier times quite brutally. Electroshock was used to get rid of it. Mental disease was treated with surgery. It fundamentally is a matter of capacity. Normally we make use of our brain and consciousness in a limited way, 50% of the capacity is just cut off.

The psychotic system, the psychotic organization is a sick system, a self defence mechanism through which the brain slowly is dried up and decomposed (as in the example of the alcoholic friend previously referred to).

This dream mirrors the instrumentalist way we deal with reality. We are living in too large a house in which it is required to use the phone. Is it progress to own a cell phone? This is total alienation caused by technical means.

It is because scientific feasibility legitimises so much. What is feasible has to be made. A holistic understanding of the life and the soul of man thus is getting lost. If it is true that we normally are only using 50% of our thinking functions, then the other 95 % (sic!) may perhaps have another function. In our organizations we tend to delete, to forget, to cut off all this.

The cell phone and radio stand for "reading thoughts". Through the dreams I can thoughtfully relate to others and have an exchange with them.

I can only recount a limited number of dreams and associations in comparison to the number that were actually shared during this workshop. Even so, it seems that this sketch has sufficiently demonstrated the hypothesis underlying Social Dreaming, i.e. that in our dreams we not only deal with problems of our working life but—if dreams are made public, associated to and linked in the Matrix—further meanings are elicited which have been broadly ignored in everyday life.

As the workshop approached its ending, the participants were equally relieved and surprised to have discovered many neglected parts of reality on which their activities and politics in particular were based. There was the view that the effort at understanding them may lead to further development of their political work in the faction of local councils. Apparently they came more in contact with the "unthought known" (Bollas, 1987). Through "dreaming the environment" (Bion, 1994, p. 46) the unthought known could, to some extent, be grasped and put into words and related to the thought known and the rational thinking in the party and its political environment. It is most likely that through this workshop the party members' understanding of reality took on a new light and new meanings—meanings that include those tragic parts that must be acknowledged in order to learn anew to hope against all reason. Thus they confirm Bain's (1994, p. 2) observation: "One of the potentials of Social Dreaming is the opportunity to create a new meaning for being a member of an organization."

The workshop participants were quite surprised at how easy it was to relate to one another through the dreams and to make links to their own everyday work, without actually talking to one another or engaging in their typical discussions. Forced to acknowledge that their faith in the "dream" of socialism had been shattered, they became connected to a different sort of "faith in dream" unknown to them before.

At the end of the workshop one participant expressed how much was still to be done: *It requires much strength to allow the origin and roots of socialism to match the reality of the present time, in order not to get lost oneself.*

I am grateful to Rose Mersky for her help in editing this English version.

CHAPTER THREE

The dreaming soldier

Hanna Biran

Project description

This project grew out of my cooperation with Wolf Werdigier, an Austrian painter who lives in Vienna, the son of a Jewish-Polish Holocaust-survivor father and a Christian-German mother. His complex and unique identity led him to deal with the conflict in our region, in an attempt to build a kind of bridge between the Israelis and the Palestinians. Wolf produced an exhibition called "Hidden Images", following interviews in which he asked Israelis and Palestinians to explore images of the other nation and images of conflict.

The source and inspiration of his project was a quotation from an essay by Raffael Moses:

> When we do not wish to face a hostile resort within us, we ascribe it to "the other". The other looks different, is an historical enemy, etc. The result is demonization and dehumanization. We are members of a cultivated society, the others are barbarian (Moses, 2002).

Wolf Werdigier painted the images he collected and created an exhibition with paintings that arouse strong emotions. These paintings point out a deep connection between images of the Holocaust and images of the condition of the Palestinian people today.

The exhibition travelled between three locales in October 2003 and November 2003. It opened at the Al-Wasiti Center in East Jerusalem, moved to the Amalia Arbel Gallery in Tel-Aviv, and from there to the Al-Hallaj Art Hall in Ramallah.

Inspired by W. Gordon Lawrence, Wolf Werdigier initiated the idea of holding a Social Dreaming matrix in the space of the exhibition. He approached me with an offer to conduct the workshop, to which I immediately agreed.

In Jerusalem, I conducted the workshop myself. There were 16 members: 5 Israelis, 9 Palestinians from East Jerusalem, 1 Norwegian, and 1 Brazilian who belongs to the "Doctors Without Frontiers" Association.

In Tel-Aviv there were around 80 participants from a variety of professions and ages, ranging from 17 to 80+. Seventy of them were Israeli Jews and ten were Arabs with Israeli Identity Cards. I conducted this workshop together with Gila Ofer and Mike Teplitz.

Wolf Werdigier conducted the workshop in Ramallah, and I did not participate in it. There were twelve people, all Palestinians from Ramallah.

In this paper, I will try to describe the main themes that emerged in the dreams and the connections I found between the three workshops.

Parents and children

In the Tel-Aviv workshop, one can identify a chain of dreams throughout the sessions which deal with the anxiety and terror of parents who feel that they are unable to protect their children. This theme recurred like a mirror image in the Ramallah workshop, where the participants were Palestinians from the Occupied Territories. The feeling that the young generation is a victim, that we are partners in the Sacrifice of Isaac, emerged constantly in the dreams. The helplessness of the parent faced with a fragile reality, devoid of safe ground, recurred repeatedly.

The third dream in the first session in Tel-Aviv:

> *I was a mermaid, coming out of the ocean. I saw a crystal mountain. There was a crack in the crystal. Inside the crystal mountain, I saw my son, who was a soldier at the time, together with eleven other soldiers. I looked at his face and he was asking something of me, I don't know what it was. I just knew he needed me*

desperately and I could not help him. I went back to the sea. When I returned to the ocean I felt I was being drawn into a well, which was like an endless black hole.

In her dream, the mother becomes a mermaid, sucked into a black hole. This picture represents the unconscious, which is endless. The crystal mountain depicts the transparent barrier. We see everything, and are unable to help. The feminine aspect cannot penetrate the crystal mountain, which holds the male aspect. The tough and hard crystal does not connect with the soft and flowing water. The associations raised the twelve tribes, represented by the twelve soldiers. The twelve tribes in the Bible were sent to conquer the country. The national duty blocks the natural, human connection between the mother and her son. The war disregards the distress of the individual soldier. The dream aroused many associations connected with the inability to save the children.

The first dream in the second session that day brought us back to that theme. This time, it was a little girl whose mother is unable to save her:

A dream I had after the suicide bombing at the Maxim Restaurant in Haifa: I dreamt that I am getting dressed and my little child goes out to play. A group of hostile people arrives. Soldiers open fire at them. There is a soldier with a hand grenade. I want to tell him not to throw it towards the playing children but it's too late. The grenade has been thrown and hits the little girl and explodes. And I ran to her screaming: no, no, no . . .

Another dream in that session was of a mother who is accompanying a field trip of her 16-year old son and his friends. She falls into quicksand. Her son tries to catch her, but they both sink deeper.

This theme intensified, and reached a climax towards the end of the workshop. A participant related that, as part of her work, she conducts a group of bereaved parents. Now, her son is about to join the army. She feels that under these circumstances she will not have the emotional strength to work with the bereaved parents. Lately she dreamt:

In my dream *I am a painter, painting different subjects. In the background of every painting there is always my daughter. Somebody asked me: "Have you painted her since she died?"*

(In real life my daughter is alive). *"No. I never did." In one painting appeared the headline: "During your life and at your Death".* And then I woke up.

"It has been only a year since my mother died, and I'm also busy writing my memoirs about her, entitled 'During your life and at your death'. In reality my son is eighteen years old. Next year he will join the army. He is not very tall and he does not have a combatant's medical profile. This makes me very happy. I then thought I would stop conducting the bereaved parents' group. I do not have much hatred for the Arabs, but much more for us. I grew up in Jaffa. My mother was considered a wise woman by the Arab neighbours and they came to her for advice."

After she finished talking, another participant started crying. She said that she was a bereaved mother. Just as the wish to escape the bereavement arose, it entered into the session. The participant who cried said:

My son was a pilot in the army, and he was killed. When I realize what pilots are doing today in Gaza and the West Bank, I am very happy he does not have to do this.

This is how we experienced our sharing with that woman, whose deep mourning did not lead her to rage but to the wish to maintain the ethical position of the Israeli army.

What fascinated us was that the group of Israelis in Tel-Aviv had never met the group of Palestinians in Ramallah, and yet the same theme appeared in Ramallah: the feeling of the parent who is unable to defend and protect his children.

I often dream something and then try to correct the dream while dreaming, in order to be reconciled. For instance, I dreamt several times that I lost my seven-year old daughter when I traveled. I was so scared and desperate. But then I found her again. In fact, it was unclear to me whether I found her or not. It could also be that I did not find her. I still remember the bad feeling I had in my stomach.

When the Israeli army began to invade Ramallah during the second Intifada, we were living at the time in a big house not far from an Israeli checkpoint. When there was shooting between the Palestinians and the soldiers at the checkpoint, bullets hit our house. I took my daughter and ran down to the lower floor, searching for a safer place, but all the rooms in the house had large windows. I became desperate because I couldn't find a room where I felt safe. I then started to dream this time after time, but often there was shooting, shelling and tanks in reality, which intermingled with the dream. So I never knew whether it was only a dream or reality.

It is important to mention that, although there were many men in the workshop, all the terror dreams on the theme of inability to protect and defend the children were dreamt by women. The men did not reach such a level of anxiety, and the women contained this aspect for them. The strongest experience was that of sacrifice: the mothers have to sacrifice their dearest.

Brothers

Dreams and associations within the context of the Jewish-Arab conflict bring to light the ancient myths of brothers and foes, loved ones who are enemies. There were dreams in which it was unclear whether one's brother is one's enemy, or one's enemy is one's brother. A duality of attraction-rejection, which can be felt in the relationship between the two nations, clearly emerged. The story of Cain and Abel, Isaac and Ishmael, Jacob and Esau recurred and were relived. The feeling of one who is victorious and one who is a victim returned. There was a feeling that there is no room for both of them. And, at the same time, there was a paradoxical feeling that both can coexist, that there is a basic closeness between them.

While the dreams about concern for the next generation were dreamt by women, the dreams about tension between brothers were dreamt by men. The strongest dream on this theme appeared in the Tel-Aviv workshop:

Last night I was in a room, in a house I did not know. There was my brother, who looked different, but I knew it was my brother. He shot at me. And I tried shooting him. We ran from door to door, trying to shoot each other.

This dream aroused anxiety and the flow of dreams ceased for a while. The observation of the two nations as two brothers, chasing each other with the aim to kill, raised in the room the dilemma: is this really an inevitable state of existence? People also asked: how did we reach this situation? The flow of associations led to a desire to amend. The participants brought experiences regarding the relationships of deep friendship between Jews and Arabs. Two particularly moving experiences pointed at kinship, trust and love between Jews and Arabs.

One participant said that he grew up in the Jezre'el Valley, in a Jewish village neighbouring an Arab village. His father had a friend from the Arab village called Abu-Ibrahim, whose wife gave birth and urgently needed an (RH-) blood donation. The participant's father had this blood type, and he immediately travelled to the hospital to donate blood. This turned out to be a bond for life.

Another participant said that in World War Two she was two years old, and lived in Haifa (then Palestine). Her parents' best friends were Arabs. They all agreed that if the Germans reached Palestine, her parents would give her to their Arab neighbours, in order to save her life.

As the battle over territory intensified, love turned into hatred. The more resolute the nationalistic ideology of the two sides, the stronger the fear of the other and the wish to annihilate him became. The option of friendship and good neighbourly relationships aroused sadness and yearning in the workshop participants. The knowledge that the enemy could have been a brother aroused a feeling of heavy loss.

Uprooting and homelessness

The Tel-Aviv workshops raised dreams of Jews who live in homes that belonged to Arabs until 1948. The dreams aroused feelings of guilt for living in the homes of refugees who escaped, as well as fear that Arabs would return to claim those homes and succeed in deporting the Jews.

The dreams regarding deportation and uprooting were accompanied by many associations of the Holocaust and a sense that the Holocaust would recur. The Jews would always be persecuted and their homes are temporary. The trauma of the Holocaust was reconstructed each time that fear of deportation and uprooting arose. In their dreams, the Jews lose their homes and are left with nothing. The Arabs come and avenge.

One participant dreamt that she comes home, and *her house has no roof or ceiling, everything is bare. Her deceased family members return home as dead people. Internal and external are intermixed. The living and dead merge. There is a feeling of lack of maintenance and instability.*

Another participant dreamt that he was four years old again, going back to the first years of the State of Israel. *In his dream he visits his aunt, who was a Holocaust survivor and lived with a group of European refugees in the Arab village, Dir Yassin.* In the collective memory of Israelis, Dir Yassin is a place in which Israelis massacred women, children and old people, and executed POWs. The battle of Dir Yassin became a blemish in the history of Israel.

However, the participant goes on to tell that he fought in 1973 at the Suez Canal, where he found the bodies of Israeli POWs with their hands tied behind their backs, slashed and desecrated. The feeling was that there is no end to the cruelty and brutality stemming from the conflict.

This chain of refugees settling in refugee homes gives rise to a feeling that the rehabilitation of one nation creates destruction and tragedy for another. If one nation has a home, the other nation will remain homeless, and vice versa.

The dreams took us back many years to the sources of the conflict and attempts to understand how this all began. The roots of the conflict, according to the dreams, are planted in the fantasy that one cannot share territory. The anxiety of losing one's home and the fear of repeating the trauma of the Holocaust, by becoming refugees lead to extreme and acrimonious attitudes towards the Palestinians. The fates of the two nations are intertwined and the feeling is that the basic assumption should change, in order for any change to occur.

The dreams reconstructed the images that appear in the paintings of the exhibition. As in the paintings, there emerges in the dreams a deep connection, which until now was inseparable, between the trauma of the Holocaust and the conflict with the Palestinians. The Jews, who underwent the trauma embedded in the collective memory, were flooded at the workshop with dreams, associations, and memories connected with the Holocaust. Social Dreaming reveals the massive impact of the Holocaust on the Jewish-Arab conflict. In our life in Israel today, there is no awareness of this connection. The connection between the national trauma that has not been healed and a deep anxiety which drives us to war was revealed very clearly in the dreams. It is difficult for a nation subjected to fear of annihilation to believe in peace.

The last dream that closed the workshop in Tel-Aviv was of a man who dreamt the previous night (i.e. the night between the dreaming sessions). In his dream *he felt that he was nowhere and felt "no-place". He felt he was not in the world. His association to these feelings was identical to the way he felt when he was a soldier during the war. He fought with a feeling that he was nowhere. This is the strongest feeling of homelessness: to be without roots, without belonging, to feel that the war uproots a person from his human culture and leads him to "no-place".*

In the Jerusalem workshop, in which the participants were Palestinians from east Jerusalem, the workshop ended with a similar dream:

I dreamt that *I was walking in a street of a city I didn't recognize. The houses were ruined, the people had left and it was very dark, maybe early in the morning. I was totally alone. Then I jumped across a wall. Here I was, in a large white space, as big as a football field. There was a lot of light there, but I was very scared during the entire dream.*

In the associations to this dream, there were parallels to many associations raised in the Tel-Aviv workshop: "The end of the world, apocalypse. Holocaust survivors who remained alone experienced the void in which they had survived."

In Ramallah appeared a dream connected with the experience of loss of identity, of a void and the inability to identify a face: *I dreamt that I lost my memory. I could not remember anything or anyone. Only one person came, whom I could not remember. I remembered his voice, his name, everything except his face. I could not remember his face.*

This dream is connected with trauma and is very similar to the dreams of Holocaust survivors. The encounter with a void occurs in both nations, as a result of losses that erase place, time, faces, and, in effect, an entire life.

Leadership

The fourth dream that appeared after the opening of the workshop in Tel-Aviv raised associations connected with leadership: *I dreamt I am in a large ship, like the Titanic, with a multitude of people aboard. The ship is sinking. Everybody understands that the captain and his crew don't know how to avoid the sinking. There is nothing to be done. The air has almost run out. Then I woke up.*

The participants began talking about the feeling that the Israeli and Palestinian leadership do not know how to escape the deteriorating situation. There is no one to lean on and a feeling of impending doom. Associations arose of two ships connected with the beginning of the State of Israel: the *Exodus*, which became a symbol of hope, and the *Struma*, which sank:

Struma, a ship of Jewish refugees from Romania, arrived in Istanbul in December 1941, with 769 people on board, after having been hit by a storm. The ship was refused access to land by the Turkish authorities and the efforts of the Jewish agency to get immigration certificates for the refugees failed. On December 2nd 1942, after the ship had sailed to open seas, it was hit by a submarine (probably Russian) and all the people, save one, drowned.

In contrast with the experience of a deserted nation was the dream of one of the participants, a Bedouin Sheik from a village in the Galilee. The Sheik is an Israeli citizen who maintains his traditional garb and the age-long customs of his tribe. His presence in the room was prominent. He told about a dream he had after his father died and he became Sheik. He felt anxious and confused. His father appeared in his dream and gave him clear instructions how to act. He told him *to keep his hands clean and his tongue pure*. This dream represented continuity, maintaining tradition, passing on knowledge from one generation to the next and clear authority. The dream was told with a strong expression of emotions.

The participants immediately cast onto the Sheik their hope of a leadership with an ethical standpoint, a clear leadership that takes responsibility. The associations led to a sense of orphanhood. There is no father to show the way. Desires were raised to receive some kind of mantra and be saved. Through the dream, the Sheik became the representative of traditional and sane leadership. Associations with Rabin's assassination were raised; the assassination of a father and psychological orphanhood. The older participants, who had survived the Holocaust, told how, as youngsters, they had been cast out on their own to cope with the reality following the Holocaust. There was no one to guide them. Today, on a wider national level, there is a similar feeling. People are confused and do not know how to interpret the actions of the leaders.

Pairing

The dreams and associations raised wishes for love between a man and a woman, especially between the two nations. This love is connected with hope for salvation. If a man and a woman are joined together, perhaps both nations can find a way towards a relationship of love.

The first dream in Tel-Aviv was of an elderly Jewish man, who was a soldier in the War of Independence in 1948. In 1956 he moved to an Arab house in Jaffa. Only after buying the house and moving into it did he realize that this house had belonged to an Arab family until 1948. His dream opened the workshop:

> *Since 1956 I've been dreaming repeatedly about the family that I imagine used to live in my house until 1948. The dream has become stronger since the exhibition opened on Tuesday. In my dream I sense the smell of the people who lived in the house. In one of the dreams I was in a refugee camp. I met a refugee woman and married her.*

This dream, being the first dream, seems to contain several vital components of the dream-matrix. This opening emphasizes to what extent Israeli Jews live with feelings of guilt. In addition, an attraction for the other side arises, which is by-and-large denied. The dream gives a feeling that the realization of love between a man and a woman will bring redemption. The dream raised a flow of associations of impossible love between a man and a woman of the two nations and of the fear of losing one's home.

The motive of pairing also appeared in the Jerusalem workshop. One of the Palestinian participants relayed: *I had a dream I want to tell: I met a very attractive brunette woman. She likes me and I like her. I find her very attractive, but her lower body is made of stone.*

The associations to this dream were that there could have been a love story between the two nations. The stone reminded the participants of the first Intifada, which began with stones. There were also associations of freezing of sexuality and impulses. One cannot make love or fertilize under such circumstances. There was also an association of the punishment that Lot's wife received after she looked back in Sodom and Gomorrah and turned into a pillar of salt.

The thought that arose in regard to this picture was related to the punishment we all receive for our compulsive tendency to look back to the past. We observe the traumatic history and all the crimes committed by both sides during the Intifada and the wars, but by constantly dealing with historic accounts we cannot develop a live, new connection between the nations. The relationship remains like stone, stuck and lifeless.

In comparison to the Palestinian participant's dream, there was a dream of a Jewish woman which continued this theme:

> *I dreamt that I was trying to escape from a man, who, when I touched him, exploded. But it is also the feeling of a man touching me, and that we will explode in love. It has been the fantasy that Arab men are the truly masculine men. Now this attraction is blocked. The Intifada and killing have turned the sexual part of the body into stone.*

Dreams of this kind enabled us to see that behind the hatred there is also a desire for contact and closeness. The potential for fertile contact between the nations has failed and explodes time and again. The dreams expose the ambivalence and complexity that do not appear overtly. The overt relationships today are of hostility and violence. It is fascinating to find that the dreams clearly raise another option.

An additional dream raised in Tel-Aviv was that of a young Jewish woman: *Last week I dreamt that an Arab man was touching my breasts. All my family was there and did not help me. I felt I was alone.*

The associations raised the issue of the sexual attraction between Jewish women and Arab men. The Jewish women related that they had never had a negative experience with an Arab man. The last dream reveals a strong attraction alongside great fear. The young woman felt that her family had deserted her, and she sought help. However, there was no violence on the part of the Arab man. There was something attractive about him.

The contact between masculine and feminine aspects stimulates thoughts about the need for the female breast, for female tenderness that can affect the dialogue between the two nations.

In an integrative perception of the feminine and masculine dimensions, we can observe that the dreams and their associations contain great pain and mourning for what cannot be realized.

The female figure has undergone metamorphosis. In one dream the lower half of her body is made of stone. In another dream the lower half of her body is a fish. A third dream of a Jewish woman repeats this motif in a different fashion:

> *I lay on the ground, near Napoleon Hill in Ramat-Gan. There is a big van or lorry on both of my legs, and there is a driver sitting inside the van. But the upper part of my body is free. I turn with my upper body towards the hill and the agricultural farm that is there. I am painting the landscape with watercolours. In my dream I thought that it was absurd that the lower part of my body has a heavy weight on it and the upper part of my body is painting.*

The lower part of the feminine body is harmed in this dream. A heavy masculine object is crushing it. It cannot move. Her upper part is carrying out creative work. However, she is actually helpless. She can paint reality, but does not have the power to influence it.

It seems that feminine elements should live and be released, in order for them to influence the relationships between the two nations.

The figure of the soldier in the dream-matrix also undergoes metamorphosis. The soldier does not appear stereotypically as a fighter, but appears to fill spiritual and maternal functions.

In one dream he appears embracing a baby. This takes place in an Arab village, at a time of war. This dream of a Jewish participant is connected to an association of an Arab participant who was in Jenin when the IDF attacked the town.

He saw an IDF soldier entering a house in Jenin, in order to give the children candy and water. The soldier was killed. It is unclear whether the Palestinians killed him, or the Israeli soldiers accidentally killed him. The pain that accompanied this story was unbearable. The pain was that such a human gesture, in which a soldier chooses a feminine function of nurturing, can end so tragically and brutally.

Stories of this sort sharpened the common pain and mourning. An elderly Jewish participant related that after the Six-Day War he sculpted a soldier standing and dreaming, a soldier who didn't want to fight. He created an oxymoron. The soldier is actually not allowed to dream. If he dreams, he will be killed. The idea was to convey a message that one needs to stop, to observe. A type of dreaming is needed, in order to stop the war. The dreaming soldier reminded people of *naivete* and innocence.

These three images, of a soldier holding a baby, a soldier handing out candy and water, and a soldier dreaming, maintain the hope that the violence will stop. The feeling of despair remains, since the soldier who handed out candy was, actually, dreaming, and was actually taking off his uniform. The moment he became human, he exposed his vulnerability and got killed.

These harsh stories led a Jewish mother to tell how she instructs her son, who serves in the Occupied Territories: *When you stand there, with your uniform and gun in hand, remember that it is not you standing there. A soldier is standing there.* The mother relayed that she felt very bad after telling him these things. She felt that in order for her son to be ready for battle, he must not regard himself and others as human beings. The uniform obligates the person to stop being human.

The dreams and associations state clearly: normal human beings do not want war. They want peace and quiet. They want to raise babies, to dream dreams, to create and to love.

Social blindness

In Jerusalem, the second day's session opened with the dream of a Jewish participant: *Tonight I dreamt that I was running away from people who were chasing me. I reached a camping site and I managed to hide among a group of people sleeping there. These people were young Americans, but I realized that they were blind. They could not see me, but they felt I was there. A boy showed me a newspaper cutting with a photograph of somebody and asked, "Do you like this?" It turned out to be an advertisement for the musical "Hair". He asked where he could get tickets for it, and I told him: at the box-office.*

The dream arouses a sense of danger and persecution. The Americans, who are supposed to help end the conflict, appear as a group of blind people. Associations were raised regarding the inability of the Americans to help the existing problems in the Middle East. In the dream, the threatening situation changes and is replaced by an advertisement for a musical and a box-office that sells tickets for the show. The associations were related to the suffering of both nations, while the entire world observes the occurrences here like a show. The Americans turn human suffering into a show and everything in American culture is translated into money. On TV, even during the most appalling programmes, there is always a commercial break.

This dream is connected with dreams told both in Jerusalem and in Tel-Aviv, in all of which appears a feeling of persecution; known places become strange. In a dream told in Tel-Aviv, *a young Jewish participant seeks his way in Jerusalem, but the Jerusalem known to him changes and he is now abroad. He looks for his house and asks for help from a policeman, who speaks only English. He talks to the policeman in English, but the moment the policeman hears that the youngster's native tongue is Hebrew, he stops the conversation.*

Social blindness is not inherent to foreign mediators only. It exists in both nations which do not see a solution for peace. A Palestinian woman in Jerusalem dreamt about the joint fate of the two nations:

A second dream I often have is a mixture of black-and-white TV films about the torture of Jews in the Holocaust and images of war against the Palestinians in the Occupied Territories. I always feel extremely terrified by these dreams.

Dreams of this type show that the Palestinians can identify with the Holocaust of the Jewish people and that the mixture of pictures shows to what extent both nations have suffered and continue to suffer. The dreams talk from an empathic standpoint. Within the political dialogue one cannot find such empathy towards the other.

This dream is connected with the paintings on the walls that point at a common fate. Both nations feel victimized and both nations feel persecuted. The dreams enable an empathetic viewpoint towards the other. The feeling of intimacy between Palestinians and Israelis was greatly heightened during the workshops.

Between hope and despair

In the Tel-Aviv workshop, a dream about stairs that lead nowhere appeared twice. Ascending the stairs was frightening, since the ascender encounters empty space at the top. Ascent of this kind arouses some hope of rediscovery, or a more spiritual beginning. The stairs resembled Jacob's ladder, a staircase leading to the sky.

Alongside these dreams, there were dreams of falling and descending into depths. The upward and downward motion gives a feeling of walking between hope and despair. A dream dreamt by a Jewish woman from Tel-Aviv tells of her falling into an elevator shaft. This is an endless fall, and on the way she sees layers upon layers of earth and of cities piled on top of the other. In this fall she does not reach the edge (in Hebrew: "Katseh").

The word "Katseh" in Hebrew reminds the participants of the Al-Aksa Mosque (the meaning of Al-Aksa in Arabic is "The Edge"), where all of history is collapsed. There everything ended. However, from this point Mohammed began his ascent.

The upward and downward motion in the dream deals with questions of past and future, hope and despair. The more we turn to the past, the deeper we fall. The ascent requires coping with fear, an encounter with empty, new, and unknown space. In several dreams notes and white pieces of paper appeared. The associations raised were: to begin at the beginning, to begin with forgetting, to have amnesia about the past, to avoid realities, and to request peace. The common feeling was that one should start from zero in order to overcome the wounds of the past.

A dream told in Ramallah by a Palestinian seemed like an almost exact mirror of the dream of falling into the elevator shaft, dreamt by the Jewish woman from Tel-Aviv:

> *I have a recurring dream, in which I am ascending a very narrow staircase. It is very dark, and I can barely get to the top. Upon reaching the top, I fall all the way down, but never reach the floor at the bottom. I then start the dream from the beginning.*

The feeling of falling, of repetition, of "no way out" is common. There is a similarity in the wish to find land, to begin from the edge, to build another reality different from the one in which we are trapped. We are trapped in an elevator shaft, or in a dark and narrow stairwell.

One of the harsh dreams told in the workshop was the second dream of the last session in Tel-Aviv. Through this dream and its associations, one could summarize the meaning of talking-through dreams and showing how one dream expresses the deepest fears of both nations as well as hope for a new beginning:

> *We travel in a Subaru car from Hadera to Afula. My husband drove across an intersection. The road was very crowded. There*

was a bus in front of us and a bus behind us. Two motorcycles collided with the bus just in front of us. From the impact the two motorists were vacuumed into the exhaust pipe. They were thrown off on the other side of the bus, totally crushed and dead. It was chaotic. I was terrified. I stepped out of the car and saw a big wave of water, flooding the entire place and somehow cleaning everything. Just earlier, my husband had gone to the kindergarten to fetch our grandchild, Yuval ("Yuval" in Hebrew means stream, brook). At that moment I woke up. The wave of water was very positive. It had a cleansing effect. I was not shocked, and at the end I felt really good.

The area of Afula-Hadera is the borderline between Israel and the Occupied Territories. It holds the deepest meaning for a link between the two nations. Will this be a destructive, suicidal connection, or a connection to new life? The dream echoes the trauma of 9/11. The twinship of the two nations is prominent in the dream: two buses, two motorcycles, two disasters of two nations. Each nation loses in its attempt to kill the other.

Against the horrendous accident in the dream appears water, which raises associations of hope for life. Associations were raised of Noah and the Flood and of the dove holding an olive branch, which heralds new life. Perhaps a large wave of water will flood the traumatic past and hope will have a place. Perhaps there will be rebirth.

In summary, Wolf Werdigier's exhibition supplied a vessel, or container, that enabled dreams connected with the conflict to emerge and to be observed. One should mention two points that were prominent in this project:

1. The encounter through dreams between Jews and Arabs enabled a unique dialogue to ensue. Often, a dialogue under these circumstances is ideological. The ideology intensifies the standpoints of power, hatred and aggression. With each side holding on to its political truth, there is tension that is unbridgeable. The dialogue through dreams creates human contact, and raises pain and fears. The dream crosses cultures and reinforces the feeling of a common fate, intimacy and

empathy. The "other" seems like a person, like me, with similar fears, desires, and pain.

2. In the Ramallah group, in which only Palestinians participated, there were dreams that seemed like mirror images of the dreams of the Israelis in Tel-Aviv, even though the two groups had never met.

CHAPTER FOUR

Life in Israel 1988–2004: associations, thoughts, and reflections on Social Dreaming

Verred Amitzi

For me, the magic of Social Dreaming Matrix is the same exciting and thrilling magic I found in Charlotte Beradt's collection of dreams from the Third Reich period (Beradt, 1968). The challenge is daring to look at dreams, finding something new, even forecasting the future from a present perspective.

There is a great fascination in the dialogue with and between dreams and associations. Reality is intensely coloured, hidden parts of the mosaic of life interconnect, understandings and insights emerge and enlighten us. We are dealing with a link between dream sleep and wakefulness, of cause and effect.

The possibility of deciphering contents and messages from the unconscious layer in dreams and transferring them to the conscious is both nourishing to our way of thinking and critical for our actions.

Yet forecasting, like prophecy, is always uncertain, as the famous proverb claims: "Since the Holy Temple was ruined, prophecy has been given to the fools". And who wants to be a fool? Furthermore, we are all acquainted with the phenomenon of a "self-fulfilling prophecy", as we are all "guilty" of projecting our emotions and beliefs on the world around us. We impose our expectations on our environment, and then interpret "reality" accordingly.

Perhaps we should agree to be fools in order to gain a different kind of vision, a wisdom that is less linear, less deductive?

The Matrix model, created in the eighties by W. Gordon Lawrence, did not exist at the time Charlotte Beradt collected her dreams. The container of her dreams was formed by two variables: a period in time (the years 1933–1939) and a place (Germany during the rise of the Third Reich).

The context of the Third Reich regime

Individual dreams, reflecting the nightmarish existence under the oppression of the totalitarian Third Reich regime, were told privately to somebody else (e.g. to a physician, a journalist, a friend), and were not heard by a group or in a Matrix as a container. Nevertheless, these dreams reflected the experience of the same social terror, beyond the single individual, and the same unconscious distresses characterizing the context in which they occurred.

As has been mentioned by others, the social role of dreams is not new. Its origins go back to: Joseph interpreting dreams for the Pharaoh, forecasting the future in the biblical times; individual Aborigines regularly telling their dreams to the rest of the tribe and making decisions accordingly; inventors who dreamt and created inventions in different places around the world at parallel times. Dreams shape reality as reality shapes dreams; perhaps this is more intense when dreams are processed socially during wakefulness.

In this paper I shall try to illuminate the complexity of life in Israel, as reflected in the dreams of Israeli Jews. The dreams and associations are from different Matrices, which took place in Israel within the last fifteen years.

Samples and reflections

FIRST EXAMPLE

The first Social Dreaming Matrix took place in August, 1988, in Israel, by the foundation ICS (Innovation and Change in Society). The "dream takers" were Lawrence, Guttmann, Triest and Biran. Since then, several dozen Matrices have been held in Israel and worldwide. I have had the opportunity to take part in some of those either as a participant or as a "dream taker".

My vivid memory as a participant in that first workshop is of a series of dreams about dead children and babies. These dreams were told by different individuals, most of them Israelis, sharing a mutual interest in dreams and social processes, but differing in age, working places and social relations.

1988 was *a posteriori* declared "the year of the child"; in that same year (the first one of the first Intifada, the Palestinian resistance) the largest number (until then) of Palestinian children were killed. Looking backwards (after a short time), at this series of dreams and the associations they evoked, reflected information accessible to the unconscious mind but not yet "known" consciously; information concerning the killing of Palestinian children by Jewish Israelis in that particular year.

Today, sixteen years later, it seems that those dreams did not echo only the death of Palestinian children in 1988. Rather, those dreams reflected and predicted a continuous process in which both societies—the Jewish Israeli and the Islamic Palestinian—constantly sacrifice their new generations. At that time this view was a taboo expressed only by a few, whose voices have increased over the years.

The sacrificed Israeli children since have been children in bombed buses; young soldiers who died in defence of settlers in the occupied territories, and soldiers who were "Arabized" (disguised as Arabs for long periods of time) on duty, losing their minds and choking for years on emotions they could not contain. Part of that sacrifice was also the spiritual destruction experienced by many Israelis as conquerors, while fighting against Palestinian children, destroying Palestinian homes, and denying pregnant Palestinian women passage through barriers from the west bank to hospitals in Israel. Those women sometimes gave birth to children, sometimes still-born, in pits.

The sacrificed children were also those Palestinians who were first sent by their families and friends to throw stones. Later on, they committed suicide as "Shahids", carrying explosives on their bodies and setting them off, while their families collected money for each dead boy or girl.

SECOND EXAMPLE—DREAMS THAT CONSTITUTE A RECURRING DREAM

This example relates to the period between the two Intifadas. I was working then with my colleague, Hanni Biran, in a workshop with a unit of the security services. The primary task of the workshop was to focus on role analysis and team development, helping that unit improve its function under stress conditions. However, at the workshop a surprising fact emerged. It appeared that various individuals of that unit had had the same dream.

In their dream, each of the dreamers was travelling with his comrades in an open jeep in the occupied territories. In the course of their current working patrols, they happened to be trapped over and over again in a deadlocked place, attacked by armed Palestinians. The experience was one of helplessness, having no means of defence and no possibility of escape. This was a recurring dream, and interestingly, everyone kept it secret, not disclosing the dream to his friends. They all felt it was a taboo to voice it aloud. As a result of the workshop, the mutual silence was broken; the dream was related and worked with, bringing considerable relief, and opening an additional path of dialogue amongst this unit's members.

On one level, the dream expressed straightforwardly a fear that could not be confronted during wakefulness.

On another level, that dream accurately forecasted the events that were to occur at a later stage and are still occurring today: the horror of Palestinians and Israelis sniping at and exploding each other from both sides of the border, trapping themselves physically, politically and emotionally in a dead end.

THIRD EXAMPLE

In the course of my work for an international commercial organization whose buildings were located in the occupied areas, I consulted with a central strategic department in that company. I worked with several executives. The department had difficulty functioning, due to a massive interference on the part of the company's general director. A short time after one of the new executives started work, we held a one-day workshop in which the members of the department were invited to bring up their dreams. At that time, the new executive (who had been hired by the company director) enjoyed the recognition and support of the general director. The new executive related a dream. In his dream *he wants to get out of a house but looking outside beyond the fence he sees a big black menacing dog wandering around. He is afraid to go out. It is dangerous outside.*

That executive was fired with twenty-four hours' notice only a few months later. At the time of his dream, he had no hint of what was to come. Nor was he aware of the director's notorious tendency to oscillate from enthusiasm to disappointment, concerning his employees. The competition in the company was enormous, but in the beginning that executive enjoyed days of grace. Nevertheless, subconsciously he felt, and so did his subordinates, that his career in the company was close to its end. In the dream there was no expression of any confrontation whatsoever with the dog. All the other dreams and associations brought up by other people in that same meeting related to deceit and mistrust. There was a mutual feeling of insecurity shared by the whole department and its future existence was unstable; its status became weaker in time.

The executive's dream also included an element of prediction for the executive, the department and even for the whole company. It represented the instability of the hastily-growing company and its autocratic director. The phenomenon of artificially-accelerated growth was criticized by the members of this department who were resented for their criticisms. Shortly after the new executive was fired, the company was forced to downsize in order to survive.

Examples from the 2004 workshop

In a three-day workshop on the subject "Organizational Dreams, Vision, and Reality" (sponsored by three organizations, ICS, Go-on, and Zofnat) twenty-three dreams were related by seven people throughout four sessions of a Social Dreaming Matrix. The dream takers were Mike Teplitz and I. Some of these dreams surfaced as memories and associations related to the new dreams within the workshop. The content of the dreams sharply shows how the chaotic socio-political context of "contemporary life" in Israel deeply invades the domain of work in organizations as well as other fields of life.

I discuss below a number of dreams containing common motives, trying to show the link between these dreams and those mentioned above. All of them reflect social and political processes that took place over recent years in Israel. It is obvious that my analysis is only one way to see and understand current events, and it goes without saying that additional understandings exist simultaneously.

Alienation—disengagement

The first dream of the Matrix was one told by a woman. In her dream *she is walking along college lanes, leading to classrooms surrounded by trees, when she meets three or four German men who address her in German. Their language sounds very discordant to her. These men take off their shirts, inviting her to do so as well. She avoids joining them. Walking on, she meets an Ethiopian athlete who throws a ball at her. She tries to throw it back at him but her throwing is weak. She tries again and feels weak again. There is a somewhat clumsy flirting between her and all these men.* The workshop was held in a guest-house surrounded by green lawns, where many seminars are held; a place that amazingly looked like the college that appeared in the dream, although the dreamer had never been there before.

The associations that emerged within the context of the above dream referred to various subjects: an intercultural encounter; Aryans and black people; a Babylon tower where several unknown languages are spoken; a relationship that was created and dismantled; a complex communication; a longing for interrelations. The associations also related to the workshop and to the events that would take place in it, to the known and the unknown, and to the fear from the language of the dreams.

The second dream *was conceived years before by another woman. In her dream she was walking along a straight road between fields, striving to go off and walk in them. But she did not dare leave the road and go to the beautiful pastoral landscape, because her mission lay ahead. She felt compelled to walk straightforward, along the narrow road.* The associations referred to rigidity of thought and denial of the surroundings, a lack of coalescence and integration into the environment, "a mode of cutting through reality", task-orientation and missing life opportunities.

In the third dream, another woman dreamed about *a clod of earth that remained uncultivated in her garden. This clod had to be loaded on a jeep and taken for cultivation to the gardener (who did not finish his work). She herself takes the clod, jolting and sliding it down the slope in her garden, and loads it on a jeep. She brings the garden to the gardener. Suddenly the situation changes and the woman finds herself in the middle of a meeting in a commercial and technological communication company, for which she used to work and which she left under unpleasant circumstances. In the dream she tries to understand what her duty is and reaches the conclusion that her job is to provide a critical report on the quality processes within the company. When she tries to perform her role and do her job, she fails to convince her audience. They refuse to listen to her. She feels torn between the need to take care of the clod of earth in the jeep and the need to stay and solve the problem of not being heard at her working place.*

Plenty of associations and links were provided in relation to the third dream. The clod is a territory taken; the clod is a block, "Gush Emunim"—literally, the Trust Block (the name of the religious Zionist faction that persists in holding to the complete Israel). Boundaries between what is ours and what is not ours are blurred and crossed; like the boundaries between the territories of Israel and those of Palestine, there are boundaries between the personal and the social (the personal garden and the organizational working area). The social culture within organizations is one of alienation and solitude. Israeli society, in general, is one in which it is difficult to listen to others and it is difficult to be convinced by others.

Links were made to the first two dreams of the matrix, and can now be made to the earlier dream about the executive who was fired. On one hand, it is hard to be a foreigner because immediately, upon speaking, you are ascribed to one block or another. At the same time, it is hard to belong; because you will remain alone if you speak a slightly different language or if you dare to criticize anything, especially your own group or company. So eventually you will keep your views to yourself alone or risk losing your job.

The unfinished work (in spite of the gardener's promises to finish it) and the organization that hires a professional but does not listen to her were linked to a strong social norm of the Israeli society. This norm is depicted in Hebrew by the expression "working by the eyes", meaning "being deceitful". One cannot rely on the promise of a supplier, an agreement with an employer, a friend's support, and especially the representation of a politician.

A posteriori one can see that the dream shows to what extent territorial and security considerations interfere in everyday work. Everything is reversed. Instead of bringing the gardener to the garden, the garden is brought to him. Instead of bringing the settlers back inside the frontiers and efficiently defending them, the army is scattered and sent into the territories. Instead of building links and bridges between sections of citizens, the government amplifies the split in society, increasing the number of social blocks.

Interestingly, in Israel, three women's organizations for peace were prominent and active through the years of the Intifada. The first, "Women in Black", is a group of women who stand every Friday in road junctions, dressed in black, manifesting against the occupation. The second was led by "four mothers" who strongly influenced the Israeli army's pullout from Lebanon. The third, "Return!", emerged a few months after the workshop and calls for the withdrawal from the Gaza strip immediately. The third dream of the Matrix related to blocks, transfer, ruptures, and to the fact that no one wants to hear; women are torn between various private and public tasks.

The fourth dream was about paratroopers in the army. The dreamer this time was a man. In his dream he is offered and agrees to command a paratrooper base without going through any proper training. In reality, he used to serve as a consultant to that same base commander and his officers. In reality, commandment was replaced by counseling, for which he had, indeed, been trained.

The role of a consultant can be very influential in a military system, especially if the consultant has had a military past. The dreamer feels somewhat guilty, perhaps due to the intensity of his influence; as if his consultation constituted a camouflage of his hidden ambitions to command. He was very successful in his consultation job, but his military past made him question the legitimacy of his status as a consultant. The associations, both of the dreamer and the other participants, were about promotion without training, power, and unfounded political and professional status. A link was made to one famous Israeli general whom the country did not want as a Chief of Staff but whom they had to accept later as Minister of Defence.

Throughout Israel's history, an increasing number of generals became politicians, often without any cooling-off period. As commanders, they intervened in politics and as politicians they intervened in the activity of the army. As to the present Prime Minister of Israel, is he a politician or a General? Could he be a political General or a General Prime Minister? The lobby of the army is present in the Knesset, the Israeli Parliament, and in the government. Previous links from the army—military acquaintances and aggressive mentality—colour the way certain statesmen in Israel function and contribute to the militarism of the government and the Knesset. The leaders are often accused of implication in cases of corruption, purchase of voices, granting of commercial bonuses, and similar privileges, and only very rarely are they judged and punished.

Relation and non-relation between people and between generations

A segment of the fifth dream was related by a woman. In her dream *she was in a car by herself, taking a computer for repair. While driving she had an accident. The woman testified that in reality she seldom uses the computer but during the last year she used it to communicate with her daughter who was traveling abroad. She was aware of different styles of communication used by different generations. Her style was long and descriptive letters, characteristic of the writing of the previous generation. Her daughter's digital "telegraphic" style was the style of a girl of the young generation.*

The associations were about a communication that is not really a relationship. The computer, an integral part of the culture of the youth, is not working and is on its way to be repaired. The mother, a woman of the previous generation, has an accident on her way to repair the computer.

Amongst the associations, another woman brought up a story about something that happened to her involving her adolescent son. Her relationship with her son is difficult and stagnant and he communicates in the simplified digital code. One day she had a surprise in the form of an email from her son. The mail was open and communicative, and she was happy that her son had suddenly corresponded with her in such a free way. After a substantial number of exchanged letters, she decided to respond verbally and call her son. When she spoke with him, he did not know what she was talking about. It became evident to her that, without realizing it, she had been communicating in writing with someone else whose name was identical to that of her son. References to this case related to the worldwide phenomenon of the "virtual non-relationship". The flesh-and-blood person behind the computer might be different from what we imagine him to be. We live in times of alienated communication; this can lead to an imaginary "reality" in which we create the illusion of a relationship which disappoints us in the end.

This reminds me of an example of use of the Internet for a different type of communication. There is a non-political movement, led by Sari Nuseiba, a leading figure of the Palestinians, and by Ami Ayalon, a leading figure of the Jewish Israelis. This movement calls for withdrawal from the Occupied Territories, for immediate and unconditional separation, and coexistence between the two nations in separate territories. To support this movement, signatures were sought at meetings in private homes at road junctions. In parallel, support is coming through the Internet from people sitting peacefully at home.

In another old and recurrent dream, *the dreamer described herself as a youngster with a fantastic vision of many flowers, magnificent dragonflies and butterflies, in white, green, and transparent colors. A shower of white flowers and glittering light appeared to her. In her dream she tries to show the vision to other adults, family and friends, asking them to acknowledge the beauty of the sight. But no one can see the vision except for her. The others are putting her off, not seeing her, ignoring what she is showing them.*

The associations that were brought up referred to a mixture of beauty and death bound together, a lack of communication, the incapacity of sharing various special personal experiences, negation, and disregard that again express alienation and loneliness.

One can see two themes in these dreams. One is a strong longing for human direct touch, with nature, freedom, colours, and beauty. The other refers to the difficulty of communication between generations and feelings of remoteness, alienation, and loneliness. This is the reality of many organizations all over the world and is also a very strong social reality in post-modern times. In Israel, the second theme colours a way of life. If we sacrifice our children, what kind of relationship do we expect to have with them?

Israel and the world—the wandering Jew—tradition, identity and overload

On the second day of the workshop a woman brought an old dream. In her dream *she arrived by plane in San Francisco, USA, and discovered that her suitcases were lost. She did not know where to go; therefore she joined a group of people and followed the flow, assuming that it is more secure to go with the majority. The majority certainly knows the right way. The exotic figure of an Indian who seemed to be going somewhere else attracted her but she did not dare follow him, although she regretted it. Instead, she travelled with the group of people in a bus to conventional places, such as a museum and a church. When she left the bus she realized she had left her purse behind.*

The associations that arose in the context of this dream referred to luggage that was lost, to the load that is the past (i.e. history). On one hand, we lose it by neglecting it. On the other hand, though, once it is gone it is difficult to follow something new. Other associations related to the process of Americanization and its effects on Israel. In the liberal city of San Francisco, the daily weather is similar to that of Israel, in spite of occasional earthquakes and dangerous storms. A lot of Israelis emigrate to this town.

Another woman brought an old dream, as an association to the previous one and as a recurrent dream as well. In her dream *she has to get on a plane and she has no passport. During the passport check she discovers this fact and has no way to prove her identity.* The associations mentioned in the context of this dream were the loss of identity and the loss of belonging.

A man then brought a dream about a trip to the Caribbean, a place he visited some time after his time in the army. In the dream, *when he arrives he participates in a religious ceremony and prayer together with a huge crowd celebrating and speaking in a local dialect flavoured with Hebrew words and singing about Jerusalem.* In the dream, *military jeeps were used for the travel.*

The associations were directed towards joint experiences, trips, and the army reserve. The jeep, as a field vehicle, represents a combination of military tasks, adventures, and trips. The prayer and the religious ceremony are connected to sacrifice, holy rites, and religious ceremonies across the world, in Mecca and in Jerusalem. There is a suggestion in the dream about the "holy" status and perhaps about the rite in the Matrix work. The dream language has been learned, and is interwoven with in the regular language. The atmosphere in the dream is happy, cosmopolitan, multilingual, and celebratory. It represents mainly travelling and entertainment, a kind of utopia in which everyone understands everyone. Those who are different and strange live in coexistence with the local people. The Jewish Israeli integrates in another place. But the elements of the jeeps, the Hebrew language, the religious ceremony, the songs about Jerusalem, and the associations remind one of Israel's past and the present, even at a distance of thousands of miles.

It should be mentioned that the army reserve constituted over the years an economic nuisance, flavoured with social entertainment that provided a time-out from the everyday routine for many Israeli men. In recent years their actions have become increasingly dangerous and nerve-racking, as they interact with the Palestinians and the settlers. The motive of the jeep is interesting as it is a vehicle linked to the first combatant units, the PALMAH (the Striking Forces in Mandatory Palestine). It is also linked to romanticism, to heroism, to the new Israeli as compared to the Diaspora Jew, to manhood, and to the establishment of the State of Israel. The jeep is also a field vehicle linked to excursions, travels, and enjoyment. This vehicle, in Israel and in the Occupied Territories, has frequently been an actual death trap.

The next dream was brought up by another participant. In her dream she is travelling to a place like Switzerland. Everything is green and pastoral. She is taking care of a baby. The working place is a small house in the mountains. The child is not hers. She goes out without him at night to have fun.

The associations referred to freedom. Childcare and work are mixed in Switzerland, in nature, in a place experiences as a heaven. But there is deception in abandoning the baby, a feeling of not belonging, a blurring of motherhood and work. Perhaps heaven is the matrix—sometimes containing and motherly, sometimes full of danger and unpleasant discoveries—and one should be apart from it. Who knows what kind of baby will be born from it and the relationship with it will be.

Beyond the Matrix, this is another example of an unreal idealization of life abroad, of life in the Diaspora that contains many temptations and also peace and pastoral scenery. Work is like entertainment; it is not difficult and there is plenty of it.

This dream may also be connected to dreams dealing with the relationship between generations and the abandonment of children, the next generation. The physical and ideological futures are abandoned for the benefit of the joys of life and materialistic values in the present.

The following dream was by a woman. She described *riding on a good and pleasant cloud, from which she fell onto the roof of a rushing bus full of children, in a far-away country. The children and other people inside the bus would not let her in. She nevertheless enjoyed travelling on the roof, but was holding to it with all her strength because of the imminent danger of falling. She wants to be inside but is not allowed in; the passengers do not hear when she knocks at the windows and they cannot get out of the bus.*

The associations to this dream and to the previous one involving the jeep were: those who are outside want to come in and those who are inside want to go out. Again, a vehicle as well as a trip is involved, and both dreams include enjoyment and danger, adventure and the need to quickly reach a secure place. The fall from a cloud is interesting as well. It reflects both the option of reaching high levels of existence, momentarily, and the illusion that one can fly over the real world to another world which is permanently comfortable and pleasant, in which all dilemmas and conflicts vanish.

There is a social phenomenon that involves almost all the young ex-soldiers, right after they finish their military service. They take a time-out from Israel which lasts between a few months and one to two years (sometimes longer), during which they wander in the world and tour other countries, especially in the Far East and South America. They work at whatever they can find and live in other places, as if they needed extra air for breathing. They seek liberation from stress before they return to an insecure chaos and economical difficulties. It is true that this phenomenon is not exclusive to Israelis, but the large-scale manner in which Israeli ex-soldiers do this is particular. They gather in special colonies; the tracks they follow and their meetings with other Israelis is reminiscent of the old days in Israel when social life was close and life was simpler.

Alongside this phenomenon is that of emigration and the establishment of communities of Israelis abroad. Emigration is especially directed towards the United States, where people work and live at a higher economic level and enjoy higher national security, while maintaining language and links between one another and Israel. They never stop yearning and thinking about returning some day; but they don't return.

These five dreams were linked to the wandering Jew carrying with him traditions as a load. This is a load that one cannot be freed of even if one tries to lose it. This is a load that is both material and, perhaps especially, spiritual (namely, language and tradition), that marks you and all that happens to you. In the dreams people were individuals in foreign places or in transit. Freedom is abroad, not here in Israel; liberation, enjoyment, the different, and the desirable are abroad. But to every place they go the wanderers take with them experiences of belonging; the load that is sometimes distressing, sometimes gladdening, the burden of which they could not or did not want to let go. The inside and outside experience is very strong: it can be attributed to the Israeli way of life or to the Diaspora; it can be attributed to the alienation between factions; and it can be attributed to our encapsulation, each of us our internal world and with a problematic bond to the outside world.

Dangers, accidents, broken laws, and boundaries

Another woman brought up an old but recurrent dream, in which *she is travelling on a three-lane road. The road is jammed but she always finds a way to pass by and to escape the jam, even by travelling down stairs under the road, and driving up again so as to be the first to reach the traffic light*. The associations were linked to the breaking of laws and boundaries, to going down in order to get up, to pilgrimage, to a catastrophe in the background (such as accidents). She bypasses the law with "nonchalance", off-handedly, and she succeeds over and again in avoiding accidents and punishment while these happen to others around her.

Israel has been ranked one of the leading places in the world for road accidents. Also a pattern of quarrels between drivers has developed, quarrels in which people are beaten and injured and sometimes even stabbed to death. In one week it may be reported "about eleven dead on the roads and dozens injured"; though news broadcasters wear gloomy expressions, there is no public outcry that refers to the victims. But if, at the same time, a missile were to fall on a tiny, remote Jewish settlement in the Occupied Territories, destroying an empty cow shed only, the news will be full of excited, righteous descriptions and people will thirst for revenge. If, Heaven forbid, Jewish civilians or children are killed or injured, the outcry will rightly reach the sky; but then Palestinian terrorists, together with Palestinian civilians and children will be intercepted, accidentally but continuously, and some of their houses will indeed be destroyed intentionally.

That dream was followed by another one, in which *another woman is visiting the seashore. Inside the sea there is a three-level swimming pool. The first is quiet, the second is stormier, and in the third there is a typhoon.*

The associations were that the passage from one level of the swimming pool to another resembles the passage from the conscious to the unconscious. The storm strengthens as we move deeper into the unconscious layer. The unconscious processes are like waves, like boiling pans and canals, all of which illustrate the same idea.

Then a man brought up a recurrent dream, in which *he was taking a walk in Tel-Aviv in autumn, stopping occasionally in front of shop windows, watching naked mannequins standing amongst artificial fallen leaves.* The associations were connected to the Crystal Night, the night of the shattered windows in the Third Reich, and to deception—to the misleading fronts of shops, tempting and illusive as facades often are.

Additional associations were about shattered ceremonials, estrangement, emptiness, and bare truth. There were thoughts about Lebanon, where we had been once young and naive conquerors, only to become enlightened later; the lack of purpose as well as the horror became progressively clearer. Dizzengoff Street was mentioned; once one of the busiest shopping places, it has become redundant, a second-rate street reflecting the world where unemployment is increasing. You look for a job and you find fired people. The country resigned from work, from responsibility.

Violence is bursting forth in the matrix; shattered windows, a typhoon in the sea, and mannequins with nude breasts in contrast with real women who refuse to take off their shirts.

Layers of history

In the fourth and last session of the Social Dreaming Matrix there was a fascinating collection of six dreams, integrating the motifs described above.

In the first dream, *a woman is trying to come in the morning to a company where she has been a consultant for five years, but she cannot get in. A lot of people are gathering, talking in excitement. She asks what is going on but people ignore her. Eventually she understands that the company is in the process of merging, a process she is not aware of. She enters a big hall where a man is lying, looking like a king, waiting for workers to finish building a canopy tent for him. She goes out of the room to meet a friend. He says hello and quickly moves away. She goes to the manager, whom she knows well, and tries to converse with him but he ignores her too. She feels she ought to leave because she is no longer needed there.*

The associations were: downsizing, alienation, loneliness, rejection, uselessness, abuse, cycles: "five years led to an image of seven cows" (a dream from the bible, i.e. seven fat cows followed by seven thin cows as a sign for profitable years followed by hard years). The rejection by three men experienced by the woman in this dream and the rejection by the three Germans in the first dream were linked; they could be related to the three male staff members in this workshop (who were exceptionally communicative) as well as to totalitarian managers and politicians, who create an atmosphere of alienation and detachment in, and out of organizations.

This dream was followed by another dream conceived by a woman. In her dream, *she is walking in the old part of Jaffa City (an old Arabic town, including, nowadays, Jewish and Moslem Israelis living side by side) getting lost within its alleys, travelling on strange old train coaches. A frightening stranger chases her. She escapes and runs up a steep mountain out in the countryside only to meet the chaser again.*

The associations were of loosing one's way, getting lost, being a stranger in a known place, being a foreigner in your own country, Arab cities (Jaffa) villages in "Wadi Aarra", a valley almost exclusively full of Arab villages in the country.

A link was made between the Jewish ghetto from the German Reich and the Arab ghetto (habitats of Arabs separate from Jews) in Israel nowadays. Mention was made of the fact that, before the second Intifada, there was a status quo between Israeli Jews and Israeli Arabs; it has since been violated.

This dream reminded a man of an old dream he had five years previously. In his dream *he is running away from people who are after him, climbing a big building, reaching the top and then the building is cracking into many rulers and toilet papers.*

The associations were related to: the twin buildings in New York that collapsed in the 11th of September terrorist attack, to delusive scenes of what is considered to be "on top of the world", to fear and ambitions that stir us to run and climb the career ladder.

In the next dream *a woman is walking again in narrow alleys in Arab villages in that same "Wadi Aarra" valley, near a Jewish town, accompanied by her cousin.*

The man following told a dream about *wandering in Jerusalem as it was years ago; finding himself suddenly around a Passover meal table, trying to find his proper place within the sitting arrangement.*

The associations were about layers of new upon old settlements, reflecting a traditional characteristic of Israel: generations of people and nations building their homes and cities on top of old ruins. You never know what is yours and what is not, what has been legally bought, and what was forcefully taken.

Hints in dreams

If the dream is always in the process of becoming, if it is infinite and it has "open ends", then, at any given moment in the life of the Social Dreaming Matrix, there coexist several meanings for the same sequence of dreams. Time dimension is distorted, as past and future change their chronological order. (2)

Consequently, working with dreams and integrating this work into our normative life requires inspiration and a different perspective, since the focus is on a process in motion.

Allegorically speaking, this vision is similar to the effect observed when staring at certain pictures that look like a collection of points, with an unfocused gaze, to discover that the picture has a dimension of depth and that a distinct shape is merging from the points. In the Social Dreaming Matrix, this effect is multiplied and one can see simultaneously several pictures coming out from the collection of points.

This work takes place at the boundary between science, art and, mysticism. Only when we are "tuned in" with altered states of consciousness can we fully enjoy the concert of life.

But this concert can be non-melodic at times, like life in various places around the globe. I have chosen to look at the socio-political situation in my country through the stories and pictures of the dreams.

It seems to me that the Social Dreaming Matrix has "matured" since the first time it took place in Israel in 1988. Then it was a "baby", fighting to survive, experienced as bizarre, and focused almost exclusively on dreams conceived within it. Since then, it has become a part of the work on the social unconscious; people have been collecting their dreams in order to bring them into an available container at a later time to explore aspects of the social unconscious.

In Israel these days, we are looking for our sanity in a mad existence; trying to survive in an atmosphere of aggression and cruelty. The term "disengagement" accurately describes this disruption in society, the attack on connections and the crazy schizophrenic splitting that characterizes our life. When I heard about Lebanon in my youth, I did not understand how anyone could conduct an everyday, banal life in an atmosphere of explosions and war. This is indeed the way we have been living in Israel for the past years, failing in our efforts to bring a radical change.

This continuously unbearable context has led us to flight. We are disengaged, encapsulated in our private lives surrounded by material goods as we watch the horrific incidents on television, from a safe distance, or, alternatively, we are travelling abroad, emigrating and staying far away.

If we choose to fight, we take one side and split from any other point of view. We can not listen, we can not have a dialogue, we can not bear any other way of thinking. We talk to our own camp members, to our party mates; we belong to a specific block. When we do meet face-to-face, we find ourselves in an endless dispute that amplifies the conflict. (I refer in this description to Israelis amongst themselves.)

The dreams reflect a deep longing for the old naive days in which social relationships were closer, warmer, and more open; when there were not such economic gaps between people; when there was stronger belief in shared values, in the law, and in the regime.

The Palestinian terror is horrendous and the Israeli occupation is corrupting. Nevertheless, there are constant attempts to stop the terror and deterioration, even though the left-wing people seem tired. There are informal contacts and conversations with Palestinians and there are demonstrations for peace. There are now women who go a few times a week to the barriers between the occupied areas and Israel, in order to be witnesses to any violations of human rights; they try to minimize violations and help the Israeli soldiers. They are met by settler women who try to chase them off, calling them traitors.

The high court of justice is the most advanced in the world, in the sense that it has the legitimacy and power to interfere in actions of the army at war, and it does so. The splits within the society do not cease. The future seems quite frightening; the situation in Israel may get worse before it gets better; it is as if there is no way to eliminate the desire for retaliation. I dare not forecast; maybe an outsider can.

CHAPTER FIVE

Social Dreaming and the birth of South Africa's democracy

Herbert Hahn

Tree that writes roots
In earth and water
Branches where it will
To touch air and be
Touched by fire.

(Hahn, J. D., personal communication—see appendix)

Introduction

Social Dreaming, as developed by W. Gordon Lawrence, in revealing strands of the social unconscious may also be an adjunct to social change (Lawrence, 1998, 2000, 2001). The aspiration is to facilitate revelation. The spirit of cooperative enquiry which develops during the process, together with the experience of what is unveiled, may also, by bringing out hidden connections between warring peoples, result in a wondrous transformation of thinking.

This is the way a South African participant wrote about a first experience of participating in a Social Dreaming Matrix:

> At first when told about the Dream Matrix, I was very reluctant about doing it given that it is so different from what I am used to. I am not only talking of the process but also the way we sat —its purpose is for you to see as many of the participants as possible.

> The process for me was about looking for connections. At times I felt unconnected but not left outside because of the arrangement of the chairs. Rather, I felt myself being held by a process which is bigger than my own issues, but it simultaneously allowed me to address my own issues. The manner in which very real links and connections were made with so many issues was surprising.
>
> Via sharing our dreams and associations, feelings of sadness, anger, and fear, etc. also surfaced, as if the process was telling me that I can share dreams, thoughts, and feelings with others whom I thought were so different. It left me with an understanding that we can engage with people we have not dreamt of having "positive" connection with. This is an example of the place that we, as South Africans, must still reach (Hahn, 1993, personal communication).

This chapter will be about Social Dreaming in relation to the social unconscious in the context of South Africa's transition to democracy, marked by its first ever democratic election in 1994.

The cultural context and the social unconscious in post-apartheid South Africa

Social Dreaming Matrices have often been found to reveal shared unconscious meanings among participants when convened as part of a conference or symposium on a particular theme. Similarly, at an annual congress of a specific organization, the shared dreams have illuminated underlying socio-professional links between the members of the organization and the specific theme of their congress (Tatham, 2002).

Dreams can also throw light on the unconscious processes at work in a whole society. For example, when Beradt gathered the dreams of "ordinary people" during the pre-war Third Reich, the widespread unspoken unconscious oppression pervading the populace as a whole became manifest (Beradt, 1985). In contrast to the death-dealing catastrophe of the Second World War, South Africa at the beginning of 1994 was on the threshold of its first ever democracy. This prospect represented the successful outcome of a long hard struggle, and although there were concerns and anxieties about what would happen, the country as a whole, and the rest of the free world, were hopeful and approving.

This optimism among South Africans about their country's future was also reflected in their unconscious. For example, in a 1993 "taster" Matrix a person of mixed race offered the following dream

> *I dreamt I was pregnant. I was anxious because there were two men who might have been the father and I feared that each would want to pass responsibility for fathering the child onto the other. But it was alright because when I told them, they both said they were willing to be the father.*

The dreamer commented afterwards that she had experienced the whole Dream Matrix as particularly remarkable because it was the first time she had been at a professional meeting where she did not experience some degree of racism.

The following year, shortly before the election, two Social Dreaming Matrices were included in a conference on the theme of "Helping the Helpers". The majority of the thirty or so participants were liberally-minded white English-speaking middle class professionals in the helping professions who had been opposed to the apartheid regime. There were a small number, including Sarie and Jan, whose mother tongue was Afrikaans, but no black South African participants and only one of mixed race.

Our venue was protected by barbed wire fencing; through it each morning, I observed an armed security guard escorting two children in their school uniforms from their own fortified home to a kerbside car for the school run. Our workshop enclosure contained residential and conference rooms arranged around a central courtyard which was solidly inhabited by a huge old oak. The tree was so well rooted as to have seemingly long-forgotten its English ancestry. In parallel with our conference, the centre was co-hosting a workshop for mainly black university students who offered outreach classes to the youth of a nearby black township.

Our conference began in a spirit of hope, optimism, and excitement not unconnected with being on the threshold of the "New" South Africa which was soon to be described by Bishop Desmond Tutu as the "Rainbow Nation". However, an atmosphere of uncertainty and apprehension also prevailed. This tension surfaced after one of our staff team was observed in friendly conversation over lunch with two of the leaders of the "other" workshop: a rumour spread and took hold that the staff team was planning an unwelcome merger with the "others". When this was voiced by the membership in a group session, the hypothesis offered was that the powerful fears and rumours circulating were a fantasy and that while there was no actual threat of merger at the conference, there might well be fears about the outcome and consequences of the "merger" which might follow the forthcoming national elections. This working hypothesis partly allayed suspicion. Then anxiety surfaced in a different form at the following large group session at which an agitated Sarie broke the opening silence by bursting out with the accusation: "I have to tell the group that Jan has physically assaulted me!"

Jan retorted heatedly: "You bloody provoked me and it was only a slap." Sarie answered back: "That's outrageous! I've never been hit in my life; and what makes it even worse, hit by someone who was supposed to be a friend!"

Jan was then coldly informed by another member that he was a "*typical* white male-chauvinist Afrikaner". There were nods of agreement. Someone else entirely disagreed and suggested that Sarie was a man-hating feminist. Anyone who knew Jan would know that he was not racist. In fact he had for years courageously and openly opposed apartheid in his Afrikaner Nationalist-dominated home town.

Sarie, who had been silently crying, now began to weep loudly. Jan threatened to leave. In this fraught and polarised atmosphere, the hypothesis was offered that the warring couple represented the bad Afrikaner Nationalist Party parents who were being pushed to take on all the guilt for the past and being driven to blaming one other. While this intervention was registered by some, it was also swamped in the prevailing turbulence. The session ended on a note of disarray and anxiety that a fuse had been lit which might blow the whole conference apart. Prior to the next session, which was a Social Dreaming Matrix, some conference members mediated between Jan and Sarie and enabled them to agree to a truce, at least for the duration of the conference.

In the subsequent Matrix, the following dream was offered:

I was outdoors. There were people about, but no one I recognized. Then some distance away someone looked familiar. I realized it was my old art teacher. He seemed a bit strange. Then he noticed and seemed to recognize me and began beckoning to me to come over to him. I felt uneasy. Why did he want me to come over to him? I had had no contact with him for a long time. Did he want sex or was it about drugs? Then I remembered he had been a good teacher and that I had no reason to fear him so I decided to go over. As I approached he indicated that he wanted me to follow him. I did, but kept at a distance. The route was tortuous. The path was also overgrown in places as if it had not been trodden for a long time. I continued to follow, not knowing where he was leading me. Eventually, after a long and unfamiliar journey, he stopped and beckoned for me to come over to where he was standing. I approached slowly and cautiously came alongside. Then he pointed ahead and downwards. Following with my eyes, I saw we were near the edge of a pool: a deep crystal-clear pool; and there was also a reflection—an absolutely amazing reflection—as if the pool somehow reflected the beauty of the universe.

The dreamer was given rapt attention during her entire dream narrative, and when she stopped there was a total stillness in the room.

Then suddenly and silently, putting her forefinger to her lips to indicate that we too should remain silent, another member pointed to the corner of the room. Following her direction, we saw a mouse, poised, in front of a small hole in the skirting. As we looked, it scampered forward, crossing the room between our legs and chairs, and disappeared through a small gap between the warped wooden door and its frame.

When it was gone, the first person to speak exclaimed with surprise that this was the first time in her life she had seen a mouse without screaming. She had been so absorbed by the dream and the atmosphere in the room afterwards that she had forgotten to scream—no, actually she had not even felt afraid. There was a flurry of association and amplification. Some related the dream as linked to the future—that South Africa had come a long way on its tortuous journey and that a truly wonderful future lay ahead at last; others saw it as a wish rather than a prediction.

By the time this Dream Matrix had drawn to a close, it was clear that the atmosphere in our workshop as a whole had shifted from adversarial conflict to an active engagement via the dreams to previously unspoken hopes and fears about the post-election future. The thought occurs that the former displaced fantasy while the latter reaches more deeply into the social unconscious.

The following morning's Dream Matrix began thus:

> *I know everyone dreams. I've never been aware of doing so. But last night I experienced an image while I was asleep, so I suppose it was what people call a dream.* (The dreamer was a retired person who had led a long and committed career in the educational field.) *I saw the old oak tree growing in our courtyard. It looked very much like the actual tree we can all see, except for one substantial difference: The tree was growing completely upside down so that its branches stretched down into the earth and its roots reached up to the sky. Everything else was just the same as it is now.*

The dream engaged all present producing a lively and ongoing myriad of associations including:

> Oak trees are a colonialist import from England brought in by the 1820 settlers.
>
> The powerful white 'settlers' are the true ancestors of apartheid.
>
> An indigenous tree does have branches which resemble roots—it's the baobab tree.
>
> The baobab is steeped in African myth and folklore.

The final plenary of the conference reflected widely on the ups and downs of the process. This included a mention of the Social Dreaming having been particularly useful and there was some expression of continuing interest in it. And indeed, some people did gather from time to time in the ensuing months of 1994 and on into 1995 to share their dreams.

Here is a selection of the dreams that were shared and recorded. Gathered under broad headings, they are offered to evoke the reader's own associations. The participants themselves mostly felt that sharing the dreams often facilitated the discovery and expression of overlapping thoughts and feelings both about what was actually going on in the country and what was feared and wished for. The number of participants, who were predominantly and sometimes exclusively white, ranged between four and eleven. Each dream begins on a new line but without extra line spacing between them so as to encourage the reader to let them "flow" together as an unfolding of the social rather than the individual unconscious.

Confusion

There was a crowd of people jostling to get on a plane. Many did not have tickets. No one knew where to go or what to do.

I found myself at a crowded conference of many nationalities. I couldn't work out the pattern of the organization nor find my team. Nobody seemed to know the structure.

I was in a city crowded with people of different cultures and socio-economic status. There seemed to be total confusion and I could not find my way. The only thing I knew clearly was that I was looking for Blackman Street.

Hope, optimism, and belief in transformation

We saw a street in a large modern city. Black teenagers were sitting on the pavement on the left and the street also curved gently to the left. We felt we did not have to know where the road was leading.

I was at university for the first time and had to pull myself up over a tree to reach the window to get into the residence. The frame was rusted and wouldn't hold and a woman student with me was too short to assist me. Then a passing young male student asked to get help and I waited fearlessly in the tree knowing help would come.

I dreamt of a cycle race between A- and X- (two South African cities). It was a long hard slog but we somehow knew we would make it. As we neared X- I met an old friend who also joined us.

There were several choirs all singing in the cathedral and three bishops leading the service.

I was in a car with a group of friends. We approached an enormous wooden gate which it was impossible to get over or get round. As we came right up to it, it slid open. We drove through and found ourselves in an attractive village.

Rejection and failure

I was the batsman in a game of cricket; hit the ball and started to run, but was run out.

I was given notice that I was no longer needed in a peace march.

I offered to pay for a round of drinks, but found that my offer was continually rejected.

I came to my regular training group session and discovered that there was no chair for me. I could not even bring in one from the pile outside, because they were all chained and locked.

Fear, danger, and disappointment

We went out for dinner. Waiters, acting under direction from the head waiter, moved tables in what seemed like a new practice of "selected mixing". We were included in this process. An envelope was presented to one of the diners at our table. I had a flash that it was a letter bomb and screamed: "No!" I woke up in alarm. I was trying to wake up but couldn't because of an invisible but heavy weight on top of me; eventually I did wake feeling oppressed, depressed and heavy.

At a prayer meeting, I became aware of a camouflaged pet snake crawling towards me. I shielded my legs with a blanket.

This was a dream within a dream. I dreamt I was seeing myself lying on the bed asleep. A man I did not recognise entered and spoke to me when I was sleeping. Why, I wondered, was he talking to me when I was asleep? Then I caught the words "family . . . murder" and panicked and woke up and was still in a panic.

I was at my mother's house with her and her maid but it wasn't safe because we were surrounded by guns. It was like in Russia during the Stalinist era with witch hunts, false accusations and show trials.

Working with and celebrating change

I was preparing for exams and also for a celebration. It felt urgent, because time was short, and it all had to be got right.

I found myself working at home but working with others too—feeling somehow both sad and relieved at how things were going; about what we were achieving. There was also an old white woman there who was being helped with something she wanted and some of the organizers were also white.

A "mixed" group were working together on a difficult project. They were orderly; there was no violence.

I was facilitating a group of people of two very different cultures who were reaching for mutual understanding.

I am back in my childhood home. The floorboards were being raised in order to get to the cellar and clean out all the stuff that had gathered there.

Disappointment

I was in a building in which there was an atmosphere of tolerance and warmth and I wanted to share this with others. But then I found I was the only one to reach the top of the building. I looked down and saw people on the grass below: some were on beds and some in wheelchairs. I saw something to eat up where I was but when I tasted it I realised it was only leftovers from what had been served down below; it did not taste good.

Some years later, when I again hosted a short Social Dreaming Matrix in South Africa, the dreams were complex, perhaps reflecting deeper unconscious awareness gleaned from the hard-won experience of working and living in a multi-cultural democracy. Circumstances did not permit full recording of the dreams, which did include themes of pleasure and pain, but the predominant tone was of being engaged in hard work. The reader may find links and make connections with the journey and transformation dreams of the 1994 "Helping the Helpers" workshop reported above and also with some strands of the reported post-election dream-sharing sessions.

This was the first dream: *I was in my darkroom trying to develop a roll of negatives having no joy. I tried all the trouble-shooting methods and there was still something blocking the process. I had reached an impasse.*

In a subsequent dream:

> *There was a small group of us trying to do the work. We were sometimes struggling to work together and we had lost our leader. Then someone who had one crooked leg joined us and turned out to be helpful. We got stuck again and could only go on after we met someone else who helped with our meditation. Some of the ground was rocky and difficult to till.*

This was the final dream:

> *I was working late one evening on a complicated and challenging research project. The deadline had already been extended. Finally, feeling stuck, and late into the night, I stepped outside for some air. Then I looked up and noticed the night sky: the moon, the planets, and the constellations I could name, and the Milky Way. I went on looking sort of vacantly. Then suddenly something happened. It was like those pictures you gaze at goggle-eyed which suddenly become three-dimensional—it was as if I had never seen the sky before. It was awesome . . . infinite . . . . After a long time, I went back into the lab feeling inspired and knowing that I would be able to proceed.*

Associations to this dream and during the Matrix as a whole were about what it was like being in South Africa now; the complexities of being part of the new democracy. One person echoed the view that while the struggle had been to gain freedom, the reality now was about engaging with the daunting task of living and sometimes even just surviving in a democracy. When someone else made a passing reference to the recent bombing of the Twin Towers in New York, the generally endorsed response was: "Perhaps it will give those who live in America some idea of what it's like for us who live in South Africa."

The dream above gives a flavour of the imprints in the social unconscious of following through with the hard work of consolidating and developing South Africa's young democracy; of accepting and moving beyond the confusion, conflicts, terror, violence, and disappointments, pausing for inspiration and pursuing the task. I am reminded of the last sentence of Nelson Mandela's autobiography. In the final paragraph, after reflecting on having walked the long road to freedom, he concludes "I can only rest for a moment, for with freedom comes responsibility, and I dare not linger, for my long walk is not yet ended" (Mandela, 1995, p.751).

Postscript

Not all who participated in the long hard struggle for democracy were able to continue with the work of reconstruction. Some died on the way, and others, some of whom did as much as they could, left before 1994. One of the latter immigrated to the UK, and by coincidence (or synchronicity) participated in a Social Dreaming Matrix I hosted while writing this chapter (2004). There he offered the following—a recurring dream which began after he left South Africa:

> *I'd be playing my saxophone in front of a large stadium full of a typical black South African motley of people. My playing had a particular sort of soulful quality, was engagingly rich in texture, and had themes melodically related to African tunes, while also evoking the underlying pain that we all felt in South Africa. By connecting up everyone through a shared understanding of our pain, there was a collective underground revolution that was being fostered. I then play at various venues all over the country, and a revolutionary spirit grows which eventually leads to a national uprising against the white supremacists: a massive and overwhelming tide of energized people who operate in the spirit of song and certitude that requires no violence and against which no defence can be made. There was never any actual physical violence in any of these dreams.*

The dreamer's association was to a South African jazz group he loved, which had inspired him and a fellow musician to open a jazz club in Hillbrow, Johannesburg, called "The Mojo" (meaning, the spirit with magical powers). On opening night they were able to get his favourite group to play! They also employed two other groups which they had to fetch secretly from and then return to Soweto or Alexandria Township—often at two or three in the morning as whites were not allowed into those townships after dark without permits. They had to be careful not to be seen by the roving police vans! Once a friend was caught and badly beaten up by the police whilst driving out of Soweto. This harsh and violent reality of the apartheid era led to them giving up the whole venture and the dreamer immigrating to the UK. There he met up with two of the original black musicians and they played together a number of times. He would encourage them to play authentic, meaningful music which connected more with their roots, but they insisted that people in the UK would not like, understand, or be able to relate to their indigenous music—that it needed to be westernized more. It was then that the dreamer began to have the recurring dream.

The recurrent dreams of the saxophone player and his associations to it are reminiscent of Freud's working hypothesis that dreams are about unfulfilled wishes and a way of enabling us to remain asleep. In dreams, aspirations can be realized which external reality has cut short. Perhaps in a similar vein, and in dreamless disillusion, in J.M. Coetzee's novel *Disgrace*, the South African protagonist, swamped by the errors of his ways and his motherland's transgenerational transmission of trauma, gives up on composing his musical masterpiece and struggles alone to sound just one true note. We all have dreams and all traverse life's journey.

Acknowledgement

The author acknowledges his gratitude to the many whose dreams, associations and amplifications on which this chapter draws.

Appendix One

Tree that writes roots
In earth and water
Branches where it will
To touch air and be
Touched by fire.

In winter with its branches bare
Speak not a word 'til buds of spring appear.

The poet above, who is also a neuroscientist, responded to the chapter as a whole as follows:

> The human brain contains billions of cells, and a certain type of brain cell, the pyramidal cell (so called because of the pyramidal shape of the bodies of these cells as seen when they were first described), has a remarkably tree-like appearance: a tall trunk (the apical dendrite) emerges from the cell's body and gives rise to numerous branches (dendrites), which then subdivide into smaller branches. These branches give rise to smaller structures

called dendritic spines, which consist of a stalk (or stalks) and nodular end (or ends) that, in appearance, are not unlike twigs and buds. The dendrites together form the dendritic arbor. Emerging from beneath the cell's body are the "roots of the tree" (called the axon); these are of thinner diameter than the dendrites, travel further, deeper into the brain and form a complex axonal arbor. In addition to their unique morphology, pyramidal cells have a special function in controlling the motor system (voluntary movement), and are found in structures of the brain (the neocortex and hippocampus) that are involved in higher cognitive and memory processes; furthermore, these structures show stereotyped patterns of activity during sleep, including the phase of sleep that is correlated with dreaming.

The nerve cells (neurons) of the brain, including the pyramidal cells, communicate "with" one another by means of electrochemical signals. This communication is characteristically unidirectional, proceeding along the dendrites toward the cell's body and then along the axons away from the cell's body to the dendrites of other neurons. Another important feature of this communication is its dynamic nature, in which temporal-spatial relations are thought to be critical. To draw a comparison, the rhythms of neuronal activity are rather like the singing of a choir, for whom rhythm and harmony are all important to the song. This may be a reason why music can so profoundly affect us as it resonates with the choir and they take up the theme; yet as our choirs differ, so too do our voices (Hahn, J. D., Personal communication).

CHAPTER SIX

"Vous êtes embarqué" (B. Pascal, *Pensées*): Social Dreaming with a group of political refugees

Donatella Ortona, Eleonora Planera, Laura Selvaggi

This experience in Social Dreaming with a group of women seeking political asylum in Italy took place in December 2003 at a First Shelter Home for political refugees situated in a small town south of Rome.

Created in 2001, the Shelter Home welcomes a maximum of 22 persons, only women and their children, for a period which varies between six to nine months. During this transitory time they are offered training in skills which will facilitate their future integration in the host country, such as language, domestic chores, and the use of computers.

Having heard of the Home and its activities and having experienced Social Dreaming with W. Gordon Lawrence at Rome University, one of us (E.P.) considered the possible utility of Social Dreaming as part of the centre's integration project following Claudio Neri's (2003) suggestion that Social Dreaming might be useful for immigrants in their task of building an image of their new social reality.

As part of her dissertation for her degree in psychology, E.P. formalized her offer of a Social Dreaming experience with the women of the Home. In addition to many bureaucratic obstacles, E.P. had to face up to the protective resistance of the Home's Director, M.T., who feared that the fragile balance of persons such as political refugees (whose "nightmares are probably best forgotten") might be threatened by Western psychologists' approach to dreams, and also questioned whether Social Dreaming would lead to any benefit for the women of the Home, other than just contributing to an interesting research project.

A highly educated woman from Rwanda, with a good knowledge of French, Italian, and English, M.T., the director, became ever more curious about Social Dreaming on the basis of our hypothesis that it may offer the opportunity to favour the interrelation of these women of different cultures and languages, the sharing of their outlook on their future, as well as the surfacing of the mysterious "unthought known" (Bollas, 1987) of "her" Home. Accepting the challenge, she finally consented to our preliminary meeting at the site and the ultimate plan to schedule a Social Dreaming experience with a staff of three persons, an organizer/coordinator (E.P.), a taker/conductor with experience in Social Dreaming Matrix (D.O.) and a psychotherapist with a recent interest in Social Dreaming (L.S.).

On a snowy December morning, after a good fifteen minutes ride up a winding hilly country road, we reached the Home, an apparently new, two-floor country-house. In fact, M.T. told us, due to water leaks and infiltrations, it would have to close down and they would have to move into the historical centre of the town.

As we entered a large ground-floor central room, we were greeted by smiling, welcoming, curious young African women, some pregnant, others with babies or small children. Only one among them seemed not too happy to see us, but when, upon departure, we discovered that she had given birth to a baby boy the day before, and we asked to see the baby and celebrate the event, she melted into a luminous smile and joined the others in a warm farewell which seemed to open the space for a future Matrix.

Encouraged by the hospitable welcome and the news of an upcoming transfer, we quickly scheduled the Social Dreaming experience with two Matrices before their moving, within ten days, the first on one night and the second on the following morning. We would consequently schedule a third Matrix after their move to their new accommodation. The fact that these immigrant women, mostly African, were about to be uprooted and transferred, seemed like good timing for an experience in dream sharing.

1st Matrix (evening)

Due to the train being delayed, when we finally arrived at the Home, we found the main room set for the night: white plastic chairs piled one onto the other, laundry racks overloaded with baby clothes, and no one in sight.

Slowly, from the various doors looking into this setting, the young women, already in their nightdresses, two of them carrying their babies, rubbing their eyes, silently crept into the main room. Perplexed and embarrassed, no one in the room felt at ease. Nevertheless we exchanged glances and carried on as spontaneously and quietly as possible by each taking up a chair and sitting casually around the table. Almost immediately the others (the director, 2 Eritreans, 2 Nigerians, an expectant mothers and an adolescent immigrant girl from Albania) silently followed suit.

While the rest of the house was asleep, we tried to live up to a reason for staying awake. D.O. started by trying to establish, especially through her tone, a contact of mutual trust and of understanding of the Social Dreaming experience. Surrounded by so many pregnancies, young mothers, and new born babies, she briefly and simply explained the meaning of Social Dreaming by relating the word "matrix" to a mother's" uterus, a place from which something is bred, grows, and develops. In order to capture the participants' interest and to measure their comprehension, she then offered a first relatively recent dream of her own (see also Balamuth, 2003):

> *Around a fountain, in the centre of the main square of a small medieval hill-town, there is a group of women arguing that the fountain needs to be restored, but I see no need for its repair as it is flowing with water, which I consider a natural form of energy. As I descend the hill, I run into some mud-houses crowded with people, in very colourful dress and speaking many different languages, all very joyous and hospitable. I am impressed with the fact that they don't ask anything of me but, instead, offer me many different things of their own.*
>
> *When I reach home, I find it empty except for a big machine oozing out a golden rich liquid similar to honey. I think there is a restoration of the foundations underway and the liquid might be wax. I am struck with fear that it might be inflammable and worry that it must be "handled with care".*

Two sample free association: D.O. expressed her own in relation to her own dream: the fountain: the Home which only apparently functions and water leaks are signs of dysfunction; the hospitable people in the mud-houses: the welcome we received on our first visit to the Home; the empty room: the main room in the new quarters being prepared for them, which could bring rich good things, if handled with care.

Furthermore, as unexpressed association: the present setting as an empty room because the Matrix is not yet born and must be handled with care.

E.P. then related the fountain to mountain spring-water and the melting of snow.

Aware that the atmosphere in the room was also melting, we encouraged the others to express any thought or dream available, but a long silence followed and we were only gratified by embarrassed warm smiles, until M.T. cautiously introduced a dream of her own by saying: "It is not easy to tell our dreams because they are ugly, not like yours which are full of hope". And then, perhaps as a part of her role of director, M.T. set an example narrating her nightmare (2nd dream):

> *I'm in the middle of an earthquake . . . there is great confusion . . . lots of people running everywhere, people from this town as well as from my country in Africa, some of my dead relatives . . . I'm looking for my children. Suddenly, next to me I see a vast hole and I feel little animals, like worms, swarming all over my body. Horrified, I wipe them off and as soon as they land on the ground, they turn into drops of blood.*

E.P. associated to a big hole in her childhood garden, which was then full of earthworms and which has since been filled in by an oak tree.

D.O. associated to a 3rd dream:

> *In a village of mud-houses some children had dug the ground to seek shelter from the cold. Later, in the warm season, from the bottom of a big cavity in the ground a multitude of black women, hands raised high, cry out their protest to UN soldiers in the vicinity:—What happened to the money which was meant for us?*

The silence that followed was broken by the entrance of M., an Albanian girl in her late teens, and her mother who offered to make coffee for us. Invited to join us, the young girl said she had too many "secret" dreams but, without too much encouragement on our part, she blurted them out, one after the other:

4th dream: *A boyfriend of a friend of mine marries me instead and I am pregnant.*

The other women laughed because, they said, "She is so used to living with us, that she thinks she is pregnant too!"

5th dream: *I am travelling on a ferryboat, I am terrified to lose my balance and to fall in the water. There is a person who keeps asking my mother for money which he will not be able to return and my mother keeps telling him she doesn't even have money to feed her own children.*

6th dream: *I am travelling on a train where there is a very evil man, maybe the devil himself, who wants to place a bomb for the train to explode. I escape and hide but I don't really know what to do because I feel it is not right to save myself if the other children are going to die.*

Then M. told of her little brother's fear of walking in the darkness, so that she had to pick him up at the bus stop. Since she also was afraid, she carried with her a candle to protect herself from ghosts. M.T. intervened saying that ghosts do not exist, but the girl insisted that "they appear suddenly like a headlight and they take you away to do dirty work."

The explosion of the 6th dream evoked for L.S. a dream she was told (7th dream):

> *There is a family gathering in my living room, when suddenly, through the window, the sun, an enormous red ball of fire advances, closer and closer. Sensing imminent catastrophe, I fear that it will kill everyone. My fear passes when I notice that among the people present there are also some relatives who have already died. So I understand that it is a natural phenomenon.*

D.O. associated this sun to the gigantic, red, vibrant sun exposed at the Tate Modern Gallery, where the public stood spellbound in front of this artificial contemporary work of art, heedless of the natural sun setting outside, behind their backs.

Without expressing it, she was reminded of the force of the African sun and weakness of the English sun, also in connection to a story of two different men who decide they want to watch the rising sun at dawn. They have a wild discussion regarding the best "point of view", so they struggle and fight so viciously that they snatch each other's eyes out. When the sun rises, they cannot see it for they have both lost their eyesight.

Aware that some tired eyes were closing, and that almost an hour had gone by, D. O. wrapped up what we experienced merely as an embryo of a Matrix and adjourned to the next morning.

Intrigued by the experience, M.T. still questioned the utility of Social Dreaming. As an afterthought, it occurred to L.S. that D.O.'s last association could indicate the importance in Social Dreaming of lacking any definite and measurable purpose, as Social Dreaming would risk losing all its efficacy and we would end up like the two men who lose their eyesight.

2nd Matrix (morning)

Upon arrival, we are greeted jovially by a larger number of women, all busy at something: breastfeeding a baby, washing coffee cups or hanging laundry, or still coming out of the shower, while a soap opera was mutely running on a huge TV screen.

We adapted to the general situation and pace and, after turning off the TV, casually placed chairs disorderly around the table which we scattered with loose sheets of paper, pencils, and crayons, intending to facilitate the narration of dreams and/or to keep the children busy.

When we finally got started, there was a small group of 3 Eritreans and 1 Somalian with a 7-yr.-old boy clustered around an interpreter (knowledgeable of their different dialects), 3 Nigerians and 1 Russian, and two younger siblings of the previous night's Albanian teenager (a total of 15 persons).

For the benefit of the new participants as well as the ones from the night before, who might more easily understand and express themselves due to the presence of the interpreter, D.O., in both English and Italian, more or less repeated the previous night's simple introduction "sample dream" and relative associations.

One of the Eritrean women immediately expressed what to us sounded as a method of traditional interpretation of dreams according to her culture:

- the water from the fountain = tears;
- the golden liquid = dangerous poison;
- the empty house = bad omen, lack of means;
- the dream itself = the dreamer's desire to help others.

In response also to M.T.'s comment that they were referring to the upcoming transfer, we explained the difference between free association and interpretation and the need for a Social Dreaming Matrix to expand thoughts which can be shared as common ground rather than to attribute a specific personal meaning to the dreamer or to the dream's contents.

The participants seemed to have caught quite easily the sense of our gathering, as one of them told us: "The empty house makes me think of this house which we will be forced to leave and we don't know how the next one will be. I am afraid we might be separated and might no longer live in a group."

After translating these words, the interpreter felt the urge to express her own anxiety: "I feel like that room, empty and alone . . . because there is something which must be solved".

The 8th dream immediately turned up:

> *There was an apple tree and I was handing out apples to a group of people who were squeezed in a car. The house was also crowded with many people, all wanting, and promising, to do something, but no one did anything.*

While M.T. said she knew the meaning of the dream, but refrained from telling, the interpreter associated those people to those in D.O's initial dream who offer what they have or what they think they have.

The dreams kept coming.

9th dream:

> *In my village of mud-houses there is a great crowd, including people also from this town. An imposing big white man, dressed*

in white, possibly a priest, comes on the scene and we offer him a special beverage called "tellah". This beverage is prepared in a huge container, and must be drunk after the peel has deposited at the bottom, filtered. The priest wants to drink it right away, but he doesn't like the peel on the surface; I try to convince him that if he waits, it will taste much better, even if the peel is not tasty. I was preparing for my wedding, but I decide I no longer want to be married there, and my mother agrees with me.

Associations flowed in relation to the man in white, the priest, whom one saw as M.T., another as a guardian angel, another as the Pope. And D. O. introduced a light note by associating the name of the drink to her own name Donatella, breaking it down into two parts: "dona" (= to give) and "tellah".

Despite a great amount of movement, of persons of different ages, coming and going, the Matrix seemed to have undergone that very process of "settlement", allowing a "good" dream to surface with a gratified smile:

10th dream:

I dreamt that I was flying in the sky over the desert, and that suddenly, under me, the desert was no longer there but I was flying over green fields and so I landed. Those green fields were like the landscape here.

At the end of her translation, the interpreter had become so involved in the dream-world experience that she admitted having many dreams of her own and offered us two recurring ones:

11th dream:

I am walking in water with my brothers and sisters and I sometimes manage to pull them out and pull them ashore . . . .

12th dream:

I am standing in front of a ladder, but despite others' encouraging words, I cannot make myself climb it. I am afraid it will fall because it is suspended in the air, not hinged to anything . . . .

In the silence that followed, D.O.'s gaze fell upon the children who all along had been silently drawing, their eyes and ears wide open. She privately wove an emotional thread linking M.'s ferry-dream, the participants' fear of separation in the future unknown lodgings, the interpreter's unhinged ladder, and she was reminded of her own regular transatlantic crossings where her seasickness was overwhelming and robbed her of her balance and security, so that she didn't know where she was anymore.

As we later compared notes together, we became aware of the fact that we had all made the same connections and had all questioned ourselves: could the anonymity and unattachment of the Social Dreaming shared-space constitute a danger of further insecurity for the uprooted women of the Home, as M.T. had possibly feared?

Openly D.O. then shared her association to the interpreter's ladder: "When I was a child, I had to travel regularly between the United States and Italy. Every time I had to board a ship or a ferry, I was afraid the linking ladder might not be well-hinged and that I might be suspended (body here, soul there) or fall in the water, without ever completely reaching steady ground on either side."

One of the children drawing, a 7-yr.-old Albanian girl, then asked if she could also tell her story, and excitedly added, "But this is not a dream, but something that really happened to me! When I was little, we were coming on the boat to Italy, I was on the tip of the boat and fell in the water. My big brother grabbed my arm and pulled me out and saved me!"

Struck, we later realized we had all thought of the present-day dinghy immigration across the Adriatic, and had also compared it to the past ocean liner immigration across the Atlantic.

E.P. then offered the 13th dream:

> *I am travelling on a ferry with friends. I'm in a big hall where I am left alone. Suddenly the light goes out and a loudspeaker produces incomprehensible sounds. I am frightened. I am panic struck, until a friend of mine who comes from a seaside town, embraces me and tells me all is OK. Then another friend reassures me that I am not alone and embraces me also. Slowly the lights are turned back on and all goes back to normal.*

This dream was associated to the Social Dreaming experience in course where the dark hall can be referred to the Social Dreaming pilot experiment taking place. The confused sounds from the loudspeaker, to the many different incomprehensible languages and the reassuring embraces of friends to the dreams shared, offering comfort and help to overcome solitude.

Right after the end of this Matrix, the interpreter privately confided she had felt touched by this dream, which had reminded her of how her husband's embrace had offered her great relief and encompassing comfort in a moment of loneliness and of separation from her own family.

As if surprised by her own recollection, M.T. was inspired to tell us about a personal experience which she seemed to cherish with a smile: "I've always been afraid of boats. There is no sea back in Rwanda. When I first went to Venice and I realized that I had to take a ferry, I was afraid to be sick. But as I stood on the floating pier, I felt happy, as if I was being cradled. I then felt I was still floating in the womb of my mother. Imagine . . . at the age of forty, my mother already dead, I felt I was still inside her tummy!"

This episode and the vision of young pregnant women and young mothers cradling their babies, anxious about their future shelter, seemed to offer the Matrix an Advent-atmosphere tied to the Nativity. So, heedless of the time (in fact, just over an hour had passed), D.O. brought the 2nd, final Matrix to a soft ending. Associating the amniotic liquid of M.T.'s story and the nourishing honey-like liquid of the 1st dream to the Matrix experience, she concluded: "We may wonder where this Social Dreaming boat-matrix is taking us? We might still be anxious, but we seem comforted by its invigorating, embracing force. It is as if something were moving in this new space we have created among us and we hope we will let it grow."

M.T. thanked us heartily and expressed her keen desire that we continue the Social Dreaming experience as a regular activity with her group of women once they will have settled into the new premises.

Discussion

Our own elaboration of this particular Social Dreaming experience evidenced the interconnection and interplay of the main themes present in the dreams and associations on three different levels: the personal conditions of the participants, the shared living conditions of the Home and the experience of the Matrix itself.

Empty houses and transfers are immediately linked to the forthcoming moving, making it possible to express feelings of nostalgia and uncertainties for the future (i.e. 5th, 6th, and 12th dreams). The imminent transfer of course recalled previous separations, but the dreams themselves evidenced how this event directly influenced the present experience, since it could alter a routine providing the women of the Home with emotional and psychological support.

It was surprising—and not only for the director—how Social Dreaming allowed the phenomenal primary task to emerge (Lawrence, 2003b), that is, the reconstitution of a sense of emotional belonging and tie to a new—though precarious and temporary—community.

In a certain sense, this Social Dreaming experience also contributed to the consolidation of connections and exchanges among the Home's guests, who otherwise would tend to form subgroups on the basis of their country of origin. Dreams, nightmares, and thoughts which contained very personal elements (trips, flights, unhinged future, etc.) met in the common field of the Matrix, beyond any linguistic difference, and evolved to the point of composing images of maternity, which constitutes the main daily element of interaction and collaboration for these women. Here, the thought of maternity or birth are not only tied to "real events", for they are also related to the fact that the Home's guests are requested to leave after the legally established six to nine months period, facing a sort of re-birth themselves.

The tension between the more material aspects (what is the utility of SD?) and the emotional aspects (sharing, closeness, sense of belonging) hence favoured the formulation of a long-term ongoing Social Dreaming project.

About the Social Dreaming experience itself, we can say that the taker's first "sample dream" contained within itself the main themes that marked both Matrices in the ambivalent images of the empty house. On one hand it evoked transfers, holes in the ground, and bad omens; on the other, it connected to mud-houses (recalling the participant's original homes), welcoming people and to the Shelter Home.

As an afterthought, the empty house could represent the mental space created by the Social Dreaming experience (and probably by the night's interval) which was not furnished with definite thoughts and which could contain something precious and at the same time possibly dangerous. The most evident effect of our intervention was in fact that of creating a relatively secure common space, capable of containing a polyphony of voices, dialects, past experiences, and memories, made available through dreams. The shared uncomfortable position at the beginning transformed into a mutual offer of hospitality, gradually extending to unexpected thoughts and images.

In the 1st Matrix, both dreams and associations seemed to express personal expectations and fears of each participant and we parted with an unanswered question about our goals.

Probably this kind of indefiniteness stimulated the dream-like atmosphere of the 2nd Matrix, in which transformations and translations became easier.

The 9th dream marked the shift from insecure means of transportation to prenatal bliss. The necessary time due to optimize the taste of the tellah recalls the Social Dreaming process which develops with time. So, as the peels must be given time to settle on the bottom to achieve the best taste of the beverage, so the Social Dreaming experience can become energizing for the mind, once the dregs (the prejudices or maybe the painful memories) have moved on, without disappearing completely. Dreams and associations about separation and loss culminate with the young girl's memory of her rescue. The 13th dream and the following association directly show the transformation from noise and fear, to comfort.

Conclusion

Our purpose here is merely to give an account of the experience since it was too brief to draw conclusions. Yet it seems to offer some cues for further developments and a few evident effects can be outlined:

- the overcoming of the initial diffidence, as evidenced by the transformation of the director's attitude
- a help in elaborating personal life experiences as in the case of the interpreter and the Albanian child

- the stimulation of individual and community resources inducive to project undertaking, leading to the request for an ongoing Social Dreaming Matrix.

Moreover, our unusual setting of accommodation didn't prevent the free associating process or a reversible and multiverse perspective; rather, the understanding of the primary task and the passage to a multiverse dimension were quite easy and natural, as we allowed for spontaneous freedom of movement as well as a necessarily more empathic trust-inducing contribution of dreams and associations by the staff.

Summarily, we think we have experienced how Social Dreaming can be proposed as a technique which can be particularly appropriate for the promotion of hospitality and tolerance even in unfavourable conditions and situations. In this particular case, we feel Social Dreaming opened a field of encounter and exchange, both cultural and emotional, for a group of deeply traumatized persons, producing a positive effect which allows them to envisage the possibility of a rebirth, as our organizer's (E.P.) image of the oak tree grown in the hole once filled with earthworms. And the conclusive image of nativity directly refers to a warm welcome regarding real newborn babies or symbolic newborn citizens, but above all to the new thoughts and ways of thinking (see also Armstrong 2003): thinking about a future and about a new possible reality.

CHAPTER SEVEN

Icons of the Social Dreaming Matrix: three experiences at the University of L'Aquila

S. Marinelli and R. Girelli

Co-authors in the recording and elaboration of the experience: V. Cesarini, C. Ciotti, L. Lepidi, S. Marzolo, V. Nanni, S. Panella, M. Pizzuti, and V. Seccia, members of the degree course in psychology, Faculty of Education Sciences, University of L'Aquila

Anyone exploring the social dream, i.e. the connections made by individuals between themselves and the context in which they function, probably experiences the context itself as both being generative and revealing dreams. There are also the oneiric fantasies belonging to the dimension of social experience, and to a person's experience of society as an individual in relation to others.

It is difficult to say how the depth of the unconscious as described by Freud could be located in a shared psyche; how that depth could originate in a Matrix that, while preceding individuation, at the same time can be part of it and be revealed within it. After all, the objects we examine take on different forms depending on the model we use in our exploration. The setting Freud created for dream interpretation is associated with a combination of psychoanalytic elements. As opposed to the Matrix, it has a fixed space, a longitudinal timeframe, and rigorous rules, and is applied exclusively to an individual subject in such a way as to form a bond with the mind of the analyst and thereby reveal the latent content of the dream.

Bion's later "psychoanalytic probe", associated with the alpha function and the capacity for reverie, shared by the listening, "dreaming" mind of the analyst and group, was associated with the undifferentiated, archaic mind and with the social aspect of the individual or proto-mind; nevertheless, it was viewed as the possibility of activating a function of the subject's ability to think and elaborate the primordial experience, first within the primary group and then the social group.

In the social dream, on the other hand, the individual waits in the background, to appear only in the last instance after the collective expression and thematic expansion of his belonging among the elements in that context. Does this perhaps render the individual more spontaneous, more individuated from the bonds that link him as a part to the whole? It probably restores him the dignity of a subject capable of distinguishing and conceptualizing the complexity surrounding him by using a less binding viewpoint than that of intra-psychic research, but one related to it through dreams, and capable also of recognizing how this complexity operates within him even when he is unaware of it. Is there a link between the oneiric imagination, seen from the standpoint of the classic psychoanalytic model, and the social dream—and, if so, what is it?

Of course when examining an object we cannot shift from one model to another. For this reason it is more useful and proper for us to consider that there are certain unconscious functions at work in Social Dreaming associated with similar ways of belonging to a common condition. These oneiric functions are stimulated in a "nomadic" space/time—that of the Matrix—by a theoretical and technical methodology and apparatus of a social nature and, for this reason, contain multiple strata of polyphonically interwoven representations and meaning (Kaës, 2004). Thus the classical approach to the psychoanalysis of dreams is not central here.

Nevertheless it could be useful to outline the relationship, by way of genetic resemblance, between several models for group psychoanalysis. In particular, the model proposed by Anzieu (1973)—the group as a dream and as entrance/return into the original maternal body—describes a creative social body.

The mirroring model in group analysis explored by Pines (2002) also illustrates how the images (oneiric) circulating and being exchanged in the group are linked.

The idea described by Neri (1995) of the group as Self-Object (Kohut) indicates a dimension through which the social dream travels by means of the dreamer's belonging to an unconscious illusory relational field in which the difference between the self and the other is completely undefined and which contains mutual and reciprocal representations.

The pluripsychic apparatus of the group elaborated by Kaës (1976) also identifies a plane of collective dreaming activity by the unconscious and its "polyphony".

Foulkes' concepts of "network" and "matrix" show the proximity of the group's psychoanalytic experience to the original sense of belonging, which once again proposes the indistinct experience as a driving force behind the development of a network of bonds.

We could go on in search of other connections, but Social Dreaming experiences contain in themselves a specificity that is not linked with psychoanalytic dream theory, the mythical/creativity of the group, the connection between dream, setting, and interpretation, nor to Jungian models of the collective and archetypal unconscious.

The main idea we are left with after our Matrix experience is that of having increased the depth and breadth of the universe of functions, knowledge, and associations linking us to others and to the profound world in which we operate. Indeed, while participating in this experience of dreaming and narrating within a common framework, we perceive the contact and exchange between sense organs, as well as those cerebral functions that produce the iconic thinking and elementary representations that underpin our associative experience. This broadening of the cognitive horizon leaves an imprint that is preserved over time in the memory as a deposit of meaning. Meaning consists, more in general, of having taken part in a dream event, of having shared it, experienced it, perceived its value and sense; of having given meaning to that which is produced without any, if not provided by an activity of listening, exchange, or re-organization.

Experiencing the turbulence of the unknown, secret, or unknowable, and recognizing that even things we are unaware of, or that we do not believe we are capable of effectively working on, exist and are part of us, leaves us with a glimmer of the inexpressible as an unexpected resource for facing the unknown—time's unknowns in the form of memory, of present experience, and of awaited future.

Icons and constants

Several constant elements regarding the origins of dreaming can be indicated as common to all Matrix experiences. Moreover, some recurrent icons can also serve to illustrate how shared dreaming works.

Here we will deal, in particular, with three constant aspects related to the representation of experience and to its evolution. All in all, the oneiric icon that arises within the setting in which the Matrix takes place has its own expressive and representational qualities that contain the notion of having originated from a social creation and from an experience of shared dreaming and dream narration. These qualities are maintained throughout the entire experience, although they do tend to evolve. Observing three parallel Matrices made up of groups of university students enrolled in three different courses of study, we were able to note several similarities in how the sessions progressed, several differences, and several constant elements, which could be useful in clarifying the above statements. We shall examine two points in particular:

a) several qualities and styles specific to the oneiric icon of the social dream; and
b) the hypothesis that the constant elements in Social Dreaming Matrices are associated, on the one hand, with the profound needs of the primary unconscious and, on the other, with the idea of dreaming as social theatre with a legitimizing and facilitating, cathartic purpose in keeping with Aristotle's notion (384–322 B.C.).

An analogy was suggested in this regard by F. Oeser (1998) between the processes of representing the social dream and Shakespeare's plays. Our intention is to point out that this element, summarized in the hypothesizes outlined in point b), is that which would render the icon of the social dream more essential and "lightweight", ready for smooth and effective communication, and which imprints upon it a definite iconic style with immediate dramatic impact. We feel that this characteristic of lightness can thus be defined as one of the elements that qualify the social dream icon point a).

We could say that what happens in Social Dreaming is rather like the opposite of the representation offered by the Wong Kar-Wai film *In the Mood for Love*. The film recounts the story of two people attracted to each other. The deep pain of having been betrayed (both discover that their respective spouses are having an affair and planning to abandon them) is gradually elaborated and, after a long series of events, a new and different condition is outlined for both of them. Just when the couple, who have now elaborated the original abandonment, appear to have reached a reassuring calmness, the man, who has so far seemed more stable and capable of changing, goes off to a dense, remote forest containing both archaeological and mysterious natural elements.

He approaches an opening in a tree-trunk leading to an invisible inner cavity and, placing his lips against it, speaks secretly, depositing words and thoughts that neither the spectator nor anyone else can hear or understand. This image heightens the story's tension by introducing a secret, and unexpectedly focuses on the man (he has struggled more decidedly to persuade the woman, who has remained reserved and silent for longer). The physical, but remote, spatiality of the clearing, with its archaeological remains, and the tree to which he confides his secret, give his mysterious confession an impersonal and transient nature. It is as if, in retrospect, once objects have been placated and deposited, there are some more profound and non-subjective orders of experience that still demand an expression, a path, a narration, in order to be delivered to a scene that contains the possibility of pursuing life as full and connected with meaning—a meaning at least possible, even one lacking in response. Is not that empty cavity, full of unspeakable secrets confided by strangers over time that we have tried to re-evoke, not perhaps similar (or opposite, in the sense of opening and not enclosing) to the scene animated and stimulated by the social dream? As Tatham and Morgan have pointed out:

> The matrix does not offer a place where difficult questions can be answered, but it does allow them to be asked. The lesson it may offer at a time when tensions are high is that, instead of directing our energies at finding answers, it may be more helpful to ask what kind of container we need to work in to entertain open questions (Tatham and Morgan, 1998. p. 73.)

Three parallel Matrices: equivalents, differences, and constants[1]

Let us turn now to point b), regarding constant aspects, and outline the three types of representations that are similar from the content point of view. While not wishing to go into greater detail in this paper, in confirmation of our hypothesis, we can mention that we noted similar elements in different contexts (e.g. the Faculty of Psychology of Rome).

First representation

The most recognizably shared dream, which can be seen from the very first Matrix, contains the representation of novelty and the sensation of extraneousness stimulated by the experience that the group is about to have. This dream persists throughout the experience and its transformations become, for the dreamers and for the group, significant of the level of communication, evolution, and representation achieved. The dream's form varies according to the context.

Second representation

The representation of experiences of separation and loss appears in association with the first dream, which gives decided form and meaning to the novelty and to concerns about the unknown element.

Third representation

The third aspect concerns the development of the representation of the experience, and contains two elements. The first regarding the dreamer group's assessment of itself: its composition, specificities, assumed principles, links with the context to which it belongs, conflicts, aims of the experience, hopes for change, and other fundamental feelings brought out upon impact with the Matrix.

The space created between the two orders of stimulation that have produced the first cycle of icons (those that express sensations

1 The psychology students that participated in the SDM and who are named in the present paper all collaborated on the drafting of the dream material and have authorised publication of their names and of this content.

of loss and discomfort with novelty) and the second (associated with the desire to engage in the experience and to produce a common representation, with the aim of drawing the benefit of learning, understanding, strengthening, and satisfying curiosity, with the need to be connected to a whole, and so forth), creates a special oneiric icon. This is linked back to the strong and sudden sensation of the presence of the others, and of the value and importance of intimate sharing.

For example, in the experience with the students of psychology, the theme of disorientation, and of fear regarding the new experience of Social Dreaming, emerged from the very first Matrix in a dream about a journey toward a distant unknown country—America—represented by the image of a gutted skyscraper. In the same dream, however, dreamer-traveller Luisa, whose real-life boyfriend was about to leave for America—something that was cause for her to worry—was accompanied by her brother. Other dreams, containing themes of brother, journey, and loss, and associations with the dream, led the discourse to the alliance/complicity among students as they face university exams and, on an expanded plane, to brotherhood, which the terrorism evoked by the gutted skyscraper in America revealed as saturated with fear and death. The fear of losing brotherhood contained many elements, connected, among other things, with the idea of having to grow, graduate, and enter adult society on one's own. Associations also emerged with *Big Brother* (a popular Italian TV reality show), which reveals to a broad-based audience the daily social, and even intimate, interactions and events of a remote community through the constant eye of television. The presence of "Big Brother" introduced an element of vigilance, not persecutory but questioning: maybe one became more international, famous, and interactive, but one revealed oneself: why, for whom, and at what cost? What was there to discover?

The result of the limited duration of the Matrices (three at the end of the course), and their aspect of circumscribed and focused sharing (producing and sharing of dreams, producing of limited associations, so on), was that this sudden and accelerated intimate social experience was immediately perceived as both a profound and accelerated investigation, but also more distant from the psychic difficulties associated with the unconscious quest of psychoanalysis.

We believe, as was mentioned above, that Social Dreaming's oneiric icons are, for these reasons, always "lightweight" and panoramic in appearance. They are rich in content that, while expressive of profound worlds, is nevertheless located in a non-subjective narrative, in a context of shared thoughts and feelings with an atmosphere all its own aligned, for the most part, with the atmospheres of the other dreams, or dream subgroups that act as support, inner dialogue, and backdrop. It is as if the apparatus for the social dream consisted of a sort of "floating" or "diluting" of materials and emotional specific weights, from the moment in which they are stimulated, and become part of and are narrated in the Matrix along with the other dreams, which are experienced as brother dreams.

It could be useful to ask whether conducting parallel Matrices in three different disciplinary contexts generated different dream orientations, or perhaps even a concomitant "interactivity", in the respective groups. The dreams were fully distinct from each other, even if they hinged on a common fulcrum (better clarified in the conclusions), experienced by all the students as revolutionary (suffice it to mention the appearance of the French Revolution among the associations of the final Matrix carried out in psychology, and the fact that this representation brought out concerns related to the experience of rupture and the irresolvable contrast between the idealized models proposed by the various instructors, shattering the notion of an ideal, compact, certain, and indisputable knowledge).

The common dominant theme was that of the transition of all the university faculties from the old to the new regulations, and from the traditional degree to the professional diploma and specialization courses, which had become more qualifying. The social impact of these changes was deeply felt by the students since, with the introduction of diplomas and new, more modern—but also less certain—tasks, professional prospects had also been modified and dependence on traditional hierarchies increased. In reaction, each group produced dreams that strongly identified and clearly distinguished the theme of identity, both as students of a given disciplinary context and as future professionals within that discipline.

We shall take into consideration the three elements indicated earlier in point b) regarding constant representations (the experience of extraneousness, of separation, and the capacity to represent the experience itself), illustrating the form according to which they were presented in the three contexts.

If we examine the constant element in the first representation (dreams referring to the sensation of extraneousness to an experience) it can be said that each of the three groups tended to recount its own particular fear with regard to novelty, and to transfer onto the Matrix's aspect of novelty its specific problems of uncertainty with the new regulations. Let's take a closer look.

Psychology student matrix

The students of psychology stressed the experience of extraneousness, relating it to their study of the psychic world: they dreamed in various ways of the problem of coordinating various psychology lessons, models, and experiences in the context of their various courses. Their dreams of journeys revealed a desire to learn and develop images, fantasies, and pathways for the purpose of enriching their understanding of the psyche. Together they dreamed the fear of growing, becoming defined, working or not working, separating from the world of the family, and so forth, representing separation, loss, road accidents, travel impediments—such as a backward facing train car, non-recognition of the means of travel, loss of luggage, documents, relatives, travel companions, etc. Sharing and inter-connection emerged in this case also, as we have said. Indeed, appearing in the dreams are unknown places such as India, or distant seas or unknown roads or restaurants, but, as participant Valeria stated, "They have the same features as the psyche, whose place of residence is unknown but which is the element that everyone has in common, since it is transtemporal, as it exists in every time and in every place."

This image of the psyche seems, in fact, to reflect the social dream's fundamental and qualifying concept, that recalled by Armstrong as:

> . . . a different kind of relation between the dream and the dreamer to that explored in psychoanalysis: a relation not so much between different aspects, or experiences, of the self as between the self and the "Other", where the dreamer, as it were,

gives voice to the dream that is in him or her but not just of him or her (Armstrong, 1998, p. xviii).

Thus, on the theme of the "oneiric idiomatic language" of each university Matrix/discipline it is interesting to point out that in the psychology group this concept is, in fact, represented as the common "psyche".

Another characterization of the "Y" world is represented by a dream appearing in the third and last Matrix. The same dreamer, Valeria, finds herself in a space shuttle from which she can view the exterior world. The shuttle's shape, as specified by Valeria, is square and she becomes aware that there is a girl behind her telling her what is going on in the world outside the shuttle while, at the same time, the interior of the shuttle fills up with red, yellow, and blue flower petals. We could say that the shuttle seems to represent a sophisticated apparatus for observing the world, a psychological probe that the girl/driver of the Matrix uses to observe and narrate the world to the dreaming student. But it is also the formative apparatus for future psychologists who will have to observe, feel and, "restore" the inner world to their patients as they have seen and felt it.

The colour of the petals reminds the professor of a pen that wrote in red, blue, and grey, which was recently lost during a journey (the professor has to travel to get to L'Aquila). Valeria herself associated the petals with the film *American Beauty* and, at the same time, she associates the shuttle's shape with that of the room in which the Social Dreaming session is being held (which seems to confirm what was just suggested). Once again: the appearance in the final Matrix of the coloured petals seems to say that the experience of dreaming dreams has by now taken on colour. The dream petals are, by definition, light in weight, like the icon of the social dream, and like the "poetic and picturesque" petals at the end, the final scene of *American Beauty*, in which something tragic has also just happened (the leading actor dies in an atmosphere of melancholy and meaninglessness).

We should like to point out that, of the three groups, the psychologists brought out even more immediately the lightweight feature of the social dream icon by means of a true image of lightness (the petals). In fact, the group being trained for a helping profession that has its own specificity, which is that of having to do with the impalpable, of the hard to grasp (like petals on the wind), nevertheless often experienced as strongly saturated in colour like the blue, yellow, and red petals. As Valentina, another of the participating students, pointed out, "These are the primary colours, not mixed colours."

Once again, in the third Matrix Luisa relates what will be the last dream, whose protagonists are two warring tribes, one good and one bad. Luisa somehow takes part in the conflict and is one of the survivors of the struggle who form a new single tribe. The participants associate the dreamed conflict with their experience of participating in Social Dreaming. This experience followed immediately upon that of the psycho-drama conducted by another professor. Referring to the period of privation experienced in the dream of the surviving tribe, who fed themselves on essential poor foods such as potatoes, an association is made with the previously mentioned food of the protagonist population of the French Revolution—potatoes. Hence the "revolutionary psychologists" discover a new system of growth, of sustenance, independent of the "monarchy of the professors". Indeed, each professional psychologist will have to find his/her own way of identifying with what they do, regardless of which theoretical model they have learned best.

Professional Educator Matrix

The students in the Professional Educator degree course dreamed extraneousness as demotion (animals), decomposition (butchered), loss of unity (their course had been incorporated into that of those specializing in psychology), and as undefined professional skill (lost lovers, deteriorated, and irremediable socio-healthcare facilities, such as prisons, poorly functioning hospitals, unrecognizable and disorienting places, and so on). This harsh representation, in addition to measuring the seriousness of an unexpectedly perceived wound (the dream of butchered animals was repeated constantly and the representation became less cruel only toward the end), focused also on the role of the "educator": the society, experienced as the container of cruelties to be suffered, revealed an extreme and reciprocal need for the help of the talents and skills needed for a major job of "purification", for which it is impossible to avoid getting one's hands dirty. The aspect of social brutality was interwoven with content and themes regarding inner "formation" in keeping with the impulse, in the dream, to fulfil the desire to qualify one's social mission through self-knowledge to the extent that an ideal increase in inner motivation is produced. Could we say that the experience of extraneousness was elaborated through idealisation (of the professor, the discipline, and of the Matrix), thus turning fear into perception of the context and hope for the future?

"Technicians" Matrix

Technicians for psychiatric rehabilitation and technicians for prevention and environmental health (two courses in the Faculty of Medicine united for the experience) dreamed extraneousness as a lion. The lion was associated with a seductive looking Brazilian "outsider" in the group and reference was also made to the mane-like head of hair of his study partner, a couple of "head-of-the-classes", while the rest of the course was predominantly female. The lion was represented and associated both with danger as well as good, but it was a lion in all cases, i.e. an efficient predator, courageous, and endowed with the kingly skills required for social and mating success. The technicians felt theirs was a "minor" profession compared, those of traditional medicine and seemed to demand new and exclusive nobility for their rank linked with modern needs, as the new carriers of health, prevention, reintegration, and so on.

The dreams of the two subgroups (Environmental Technicians and Technicians for Psychiatric Rehabilitation) were quite distinct from each other, and clearly "partisan": a truck selling hotdogs and french fries on a broad green meadow opened the series of the environmental technicians (images of impotence, such as being unable to move with feet stuck in cement, falling into darkness or extreme temperatures, not recognising landscapes or cities either of other eras or else nonsensical or unstable, and so on).

Difficult, disrupted pathways posing the problems of human degradation, alienation, and enigma, opened the parallel series dreamt by psychiatric rehabilitation technicians (scary and troubled journeys, through complex and unknown landscapes, contact with alienating and unexpected people, objects, and situations that introduced incongruence and mystery).

These dreams linked up together, like a sort of train, until they reached more synthetic and harmonious images oriented towards hope and more realistic evaluations: as if the experience of dreaming together, of shared thoughts and intimate contact such as no one had foreseen, had produced a comforting sense of novelty associated with an increase in the awareness and sense of the self as belonging to the category of student and professional, cohesive, rooted, and endowed with a recognizable identity. In one particularly effective dream the dreamer finds himself in an unknown country in an apparently different era with the unusual customs and fashions—gendarmes in 19th century uniforms and other stylised personages—associated with the fairy tale characters of *Pinocchio*, the wooden doll who becomes a real boy after a long series of mishaps.

The dream speaks of memories of other lives lived in other unknown and distant times and spaces, and was experienced as the possibility of creating a scenario "other" than that of the accelerated pace of the Faculty of Medicine, which steals subjective and real time requiring not dreams and thoughts but concrete production, exams, study time, etc., before being able to become doctors—or "real boys".

Another association that recalls the dark period overtones of the film *Jack the Ripper*, which has recently been shown on TV, seemed to allude to the "ripper" lion of the first dream and to the theme of a doctor/surgeon who cuts—(technicians, as opposed to doctors, do not perform this task).

Could we say that dreaming was becoming an opportunity for newfound awareness?

Difference or identities

It is not, however, sufficient to speak about the differences in identity of the three Matrices. We should rather say that the differences were born of an equalizing tendency, experienced as a form of terrorism, and that dreaming the difference was the treatment by which the dreamers were able to survive the nightmare.

This equality had revealed, in dreaming together at the university, a shared nightmare: the nightmare that the world in which they were about to be born as adults was a world dominated by lions (the Americans) and by butchered animals (the Third World), where skyscrapers were gutted, brothers lost forever, and certainties eliminated, to the point that finding and identifying oneself was impossible. In addition to personal representations, this collective dream was associated with the imagination of a broader social group and bore witness to the fact that the space of one's generation, one's destiny, one's city, was also part of other orbits linked with the dreams and destinies of other persons distant in space and time.

The very name of this university city—L'Aquila ("The Eagle" in English)—seemed to encourage a tendency to dream of hunting animals (lions) and prey (butchered animals) and to be associated with its imperial origins (the eagle was the symbol chosen by Emperor Frederic II). The emperor intended the city as the glorious and noble juncture of all the surrounding fiefdoms, the various features of which he wished to reproduce and maintain: family crests, edifices, fountains, churches, 99 in number as was the number of the surrounding hilltop castles. To this day in the most ancient part of the city one can still see the fountain of the 99 spouts recalling these origins. It could be that L'Aquila's rebirth as a university town, and that of the socially more modern and competitive faculties, sparked in the Matrices dreams of glory (and impotence), of superiority (and cruelty), of aggressiveness (and fear), belonging to the historic past. And it could also be that in this way the dreamers tended to express the contradiction of their own city between strong primitive ritualistic traditions and the new modern and technological organization. Perhaps the students are expecting a response to this painful contradiction from the university—in fact, they are demanding it.

In all three cases the reaction to the discovery of things in common, of bonds formed so deeply and so rapidly, was very keen—something so precious that is there and yet none of which one is conscious until they come to use it. In all three cases the anxiety associated with novelty and the discovery of a nightmare were elaborated in the context of differentiated and specific relational and thought systems that went on to evolve towards a cognitive and reassuring form. No one was aware of having produced such a precise and disturbing social representation on their own, but everyone was aware of having participated in it and of having shared it: courage revealed in the midst of terror and doubt. We noted, along with the students that contributed to the reorganization of dreams and in drafting this article, that the participant who had launched the first Matrix with the first dream (the gutted skyscraper), had been the same one to close it, by recounting the last dream (the warring tribes and the surviving tribe). In our opinion, this element could have something to do with the idea that the Social Dreaming discourse has evidently blazed and followed its own trail.

In the words of V. Cesarini, C. Ciotti, L. Lepidi, S. Marzolo, V. Nanni, S. Panella, M. Pizzuti, and V. Seccia, participants in the psychology Matrix and in writing this article, "The possibility of coming into contact with knowledge and awareness different from that to which the students were accustomed, destabilised them and undermined the security they had achieved." Social Dreaming was, however, a fundamental experience since it led to the formation of a group of survivors (the persons who worked on the re-elaboration of the three Matrices), who are emblematic of the evolution of a long process of growth.

CHAPTER EIGHT

Shedding light on organizational shadows

Helen Morgan

Introduction

Social Dreaming was first conceptualized in the early 1980s by W. Gordon Lawrence, then a member of London's Tavistock Institute of Human Relations. Social Dreaming programmes have since taken place in many countries including Britain, Germany, Israel, Sweden, Australia, and the United States. It is a pioneering methodology that addresses the unthought and unconscious dimensions of the social world. It is based on the assumption that we dream not just for ourselves, but as part of the larger context in which we live. This perspective regards dreams as more than the private possession of the dreamer, but as also relevant to social reality. This idea has an ancient lineage. Long before Freud and Jung began to study dreams, dreams and dreaming had great significance to people in societies such as the Australian Aboriginals, Native Americans, African groups, etc., as they attempted to understand the meaning of their lives and the world in which they lived.

Social Dreaming

The Social Dreaming Matrix is a special kind of container which is set up and maintained in a manner that maximizes free association

This paper was first published in the BAP Journal, No. 2, Vol. 40, July 2002.

to the images offered by the dreams. It seems to take away the emphasis on the individual ego and allows us to let go a little of the need to perform and the problems of persona. By "losing" the ego in the Matrix, proper attention can be paid to the dreams and, hence to the unconscious of the group. Thus a deeper, more democratic dynamic can emerge.

Our view of organizations too often is constrained by the observable, logical, and rational. It frequently relies on theories and strategies designed to maintain control over outcomes—even in the midst of turbulence, complexity, and unpredictability. Despite this, the dynamics hidden in the shadows typically present the most challenges for those working with and in organizations. An exploration of what is unspoken, tacit, and presumably unknown, can reveal shared fears, fantasies, and conflicts and thereby provide a deeper understanding of organizational reality.

No organization can operate without the conscious ego activities concerning policy making, management, representing, negotiating, and decision making. These belong to the realm of ego functioning, but all risk clashes of personality, power struggles, inflation, matters of kudos, etc. The Social Dreaming Matrix can provide a very different sort of space where the same personnel can engage with each other in a very different context, which promotes collaboration in exploring uncertainty and paradox. As we know from individual analysis, the dream presents us with what is, rather than what "ought to be" and therefore offers the expression of shadow material within a framework which is not restricted by morality, judgement, or superego.

The central task of the Matrix as given at the commencement of each Matrix by one or other of the convenors is *to transform thinking by associating to the dreams made available to the Matrix in order to make links and find connections between private thought and social meaning*. The question arises of the nature of the dream itself and, more especially, whose dream it is. For the approach to the dream offered within the context of the Matrix is different to that when the dream is presented within an individual analysis. In the latter case the interest is in the associations of the dreamer and, possibly, of the analyst—at least in the countertransference. The dream, and all aspects within it, are regarded as a communication of the different aspects of that individual's particular psyche, and possibly of that particular transference. How the dream may be interpreted will be viewed differently depending on one's theoretical position but, on the whole, the dream will be seen as belonging to the dreamer.

In the Matrix a different approach is taken in that any dream which is spoken of within the Matrix, then belongs to the Matrix. The personal relevance and meaning for the person who brings the dream may be explored and interpreted privately elsewhere, but in the Matrix those personal implications are avoided—indeed one of the tasks of the convenors is to ensure that such work does not go on within the Matrix. Instead the dream is taken up as belonging to all, and played with, associated to, thought about as such.

The central point is that individual analysis offers one sort of container for the dream and is worked with from one set of assumptions. The Social Dreaming Matrix offers another sort of container and works from a different set. A question arises as to whether, if the container changes, then are different dreams dreamt? Lawrence maintains:

> To take the same thought processes as are used in psychoanalysis into a Social Dreaming Matrix is not valid because, it is my hypothesis, a different version or even type of dream is evoked. More particularly, if the container system for receiving the dream is changed, the dream-contained will change . . . . More and more I begin to accept Bion's notion that we have to be available for thought—the notion that there are thoughts in search of a thinker. Can we extend this to think in terms of dreams in search of a dreamer? What I think the Social Dreaming Matrix questions is the ideology that dreams belong to a person and are to be interpreted as such. This is not to devalue that kind of work—so important for myself in my own psychoanalysis. All I am saying is that the matrix produces different kinds of dreams through dreamers. The context is different, that is all (Lawrence, 1998. pp. 31–33).

"Changing times": Social Dreaming in Oxford, September, 2001

The British Association of Psychotherapists (BAP) is an independent psychotherapy training organization established in 1951. It comprises three sections: Child and Adolescent, Jungian Analytic, and Psychoanalytic. Each section runs a distinct training although much post-qualification professional development is cross-sectional. In September 2001 a 50th Anniversary Residential Conference was held in Oxford entitled "Changing Times". As part of this conference I, a member of the Jungian Analytic section, and Mannie Sher, a member of the Psychoanalytic section, offered to convene a Social Dreaming Matrix as a means of providing a container to hold both the conflict and creativity of the weekend. We held three Matrices, each of an hour's duration, on Friday evening and on Saturday and Sunday mornings at 8.00 a.m. The room had chairs arranged in a spiral facing inwards. Part of the information that was given to all conference participants concerning the matrix is as follows:

> This is an important time for the BAP . . . For the duration of the conference we will speak, listen, think and discuss. We will also dream. What might these dreams tell us about the nature of the organizational, professional. and social contexts in which we find ourselves? The Matrix provides a different container for the dream than that used conventionally, and thus shifts the focus from the dreamer to the dream itself, thus allowing the possibility of an exploration of these wider contexts. Over the weekend our work will incorporate dreams, metaphors, and myths to help us gain a deeper understanding of what is left obscure in our organizational work.
>
> The primary task of the event will be to associate to one's own and other participants' dreams which are made available to the Matrix so as to make links and find connections. The Matrix is entirely voluntary. It will not be necessary to bring a dream to take part, nor will individuals be required to participate at every session. No previous experience or knowledge is necessary—anyone interested in better understanding the deeper dynamics of organizations is welcome. We invite you to join us in our exploration. (Convenors: Helen Morgan and Mannie Sher).

It is difficult to give an account of the events of a series of Social Dreaming Matrices. Each individual exists as a nodal point in a network during the life of the Matrix and where you are located in this net determines your experience and your memory, which means that there will be as many impressions and associations as there were participants. The following is an attempt to give some flavour of the experience as seen by the convenors using a few dreams by way of illustrating some of the themes that emerged. Perhaps a starting point is to note the timing of this event in relation to world events.

There is always a certain anxiety prior to convening a Matrix as it is such an unknown quantity and, unlike giving a paper or a workshop, there is only a limited amount of preparation work that one can do. As convenors we talked together on a number of occasions both aware that our role was to attend to the Matrix as container so that what might need to be contained could enter. In previous discussions with W. Gordon Lawrence, he had offered the mantra, "trust the Matrix." So far experience had proved him right, but thoughts still did turn to the differences and conflicts within the BAP the Matrix might be called on to hold.

Then, ten days before the conference was due to begin, the terrorist attacks in America took place. Suddenly it looked as though more than the parochial concerns of one psychotherapy organization would strain the containing function of the Matrix. On Thursday night, September 20th, prior to driving to Oxford on the Friday and the first Matrix, I had the following dream:

> *I am convening the Matrix but there seems to be a "higher power" who has set us a task which is told to me and which I take back to the Matrix. It seems we have to name the two planes that flew into the twin towers. At first I don't believe we can and am surprised and relieved when we achieve it (I don't recall what the names were). It seems that future war or peace will depend on this task. However, when I return with the answer, I am told that was just a warm-up. The real task is to come to a consensus about what has happened and what the right feelings are. Now I panic as I realiZe that there is no way we can agree on this. I try asking whether the statement "two planes flew into the twin towers" will do, but am not surprised by the reply that it is the feeling tone we have to agree on. I am despondent.*

Any dreams we have as convenors we do not offer to the Matrix as they can skew the work. We do, however, discuss them together seeing them as communications concerning the Matrix as well as our role as convenors. This dream seemed to be saying something about the need to name, but the need, also to take this beyond naming. We also saw how the Matrix would have to hold possibly very different feelings about what happened on September 11th and, other than the barest of descriptions, no consensus can be reached. We also noted the inflation of assuming the events of the Matrix could decide world affairs. Thinking of how the dream may operate at a number of levels, ideas occurred around the "twin towers" of Freud and Jung and the implications for the BAP.

In the Matrix itself, the impact of the world events the week before echoed through the dreams and around the Matrix. One dream that was returned to a number of times throughout the weekend was related very early on in the first Matrix. The dreamer was in a group singing "Onward Christian Soldiers". Some members were singing loudly and with gusto, others didn't know the words and were trying to hum along. Here was the idea of "Christian soldiers marching as to war", the division between those who were in the know and those who could only hum along and pretend they knew the words, and the concept of the Crusades.

There were a number of references in the dreams and in the associations to the split between Freud and Jung. Someone dreamt of the quadrangle in the college we were staying in which had flagstones with rings in. The dreamer pulled up the flagstones to find embers smouldering with human remains which had been there hundreds of years. References were then made to a similar motif in a dream Jung told Freud which they both interpreted very differently, and which played its part in the breakdown of their friendship.

Other motifs related to concerns about the BAP itself and to analytic work generally. Anxiety about the future was evident in a number of the dreams. Also many dreams featured those who were now dead, husbands, loved ones, analysts .... Lawrence writes:

> For myself, I think of the individuals in the Matrix each with their personal world of other individuals alive and dead, so that the Matrix is full of the shades of biographies (the dead are alive) (Lawrence, 1998, p. 32).

The "ancestors" of the BAP were certainly there in the Matrices, not just Freud and Jung, but also Winnicott, Klein, Bion. And also the more direct personal ancestors—the founders of the association and their dream. How, at our 50th birthday party were we to say goodbye with gratitude to them and their dream and allow our own?

As is the way of the Matrix, such *gravitas* seem often to be balanced by the more light-hearted. After all this weighty talk someone brought a dream that we were all in the refectory in the evening. There had been a banquet but now the tables were cleared away for dancing. There was even a mirror-ball. The dreamer started singing and everyone joined in. The song was the Beatles number which started "Close your eyes and I'll kiss you. . . ." Associations to this dream led down a complex track to "Don't throw your love away" and ended, perhaps inevitably with "Yesterday".

End point

In the Matrix there is no requirement to come to a conclusion or to make a decision. We do not need to agree on an interpretation of a dream or of the unconscious dynamics of an individual or of the group. The central currency is that of the dream, and the language is image and metaphor. The space expands to contain what Lawrence describes as a "multiverse" of meanings allowing participants to play with the associations that arise. Because issues of power, authority, and responsibility are not the business of the Matrix except as they are dreamt of, and because the role of the dreamer and of the person offering an association is a democratic one, the individual can work outside of the persona and a sense of *communitas* may develop. The "problems" are provided, not by the conscious ego but by the images of the dream and this can allow the lessening of tensions between individuals and "positions". Thus something more unconscious, more collective may have voice. In Bion's terms, participants make themselves available for thought, and this ponderous space allows the emergence, not of conclusions, but of images, associations, symbols, and ideas.

CHAPTER NINE

Social Dreaming at the Jung Congress

Peter Tatham

In 1995, the International Association for Analytical Psychology held its 13th triennial Congress in Zürich, Jung's hometown. Seven hundred analysts and students attended. My colleague Helen Morgan and I had offered to convene a Social Dreaming Matrix as part of the programme, which offer had been accepted. We led the Matrix, for an hour, each morning, before the beginning of the day's more formal offerings; and had been given a large ground floor hall, with floor to ceiling windows of plate glass to work in. It looked out onto a busy street and Lake Zürich as well. We sat on metal stacking chairs, and since we had not expected as many people to attend (about a hundred), latecomers had to take more chairs from the stack, with much noise. That, as well as the heavy entrance door, banging shut whenever someone entered late (which many did), made for a noisy start. One person asked angrily if we couldn't lock the door so that latecomers could not enter and disturb us. However, since the title of the congress was "Open Questions in Jungian Psychology", Helen wondered aloud if such an understandable wish to close and lock the door also expressed the general difficulty with keeping all sorts of other things "open"—such as the "questions" of our title—that we had come to Zürich to think about, together. At the end of that first session, I inexplicably closed the Matrix ten minutes early. Amid laughter we agreed that even convenors could have difficulty in keeping things open.

Overall, the Matrix was popular, despite language difficulties, for not everyone was fluent in English. One of the official "simultaneous translators" read of it in the programme and had asked if she might also attend; and did so, making some useful interventions. Later we recognised that the language of dreams was a shared *lingua franca*, but individual meanings could not be translated.

Since the hall that was used for the main daily lectures was directly above us, someone talked of our work as being "in the basement", a phrase suggesting that our task included an underpinning of each day's more intellectual fare, above us. This was a helpful image and the Matrix was an undoubted success (Tatham & Morgan, 1997 in Lawrence, 1998).

Three years later, Helen and another colleague equally successfully convened a Social Dreaming Matrix at the Florence Congress in 1998. And, after another three years, Helen and I led Social Dreaming together once more, when the International Association of Analytic Psychology met in England, at Cambridge, under the catch-all title of: "2001". That Matrix is the subject of this chapter. The congress title suggested not only a fresh millennium, but also, perhaps, new beginnings for our association, whose membership numbers were swelling and which now had five official languages.

Our previous work with Social Dreaming had shown us that providing time for an expression of "the unconscious" within such large and mostly intellectually or politically minded congresses, before the day's main business began, undoubtedly acted as a useful counter-balance to the diverse fullness, and intensity, of any formal programme of lectures, seminars, and workshops. The remainder of this chapter tries to show, in greater detail, how that value of providing a space for Social Dreaming at such large events is expressed, in various ways relevant to the particular nature of that event.

At Cambridge, the setting we were given, in which to hold the Matrix, was the city's Guildhall: a large, high space, more used to public events and orchestral performance than for a quiet telling of our night-time dreams. With its concert hall size, high-vaulted ceiling, and the neo-classical formality of its decoration, it was not an obvious venue for shared intimacies. Yet a hundred or so people attended, on five mornings, bringing their images and associations to our spiral of chairs, just sitting in which, we felt dwarfed by the intimidating space around us. The acoustics of the hall were against us too, so that on several occasions, frustrated individuals got up and left the Matrix, angrily complaining that hearing what others were saying was too difficult. As a result of these defections, we did agree to switch off the air-conditioning, but resisted all demands, however persistent, to find another room. Knowing, from our experience of Social Dreaming that everything which happened, or was spoken of within the Matrix belonged to it, we suggested instead that the form of any such congress of several hundred people, with various contributions programmed at the same time, in five official languages, inevitably meant that no individual could hear everything on the programme. Nor could he or she find it easy to make their responses "heard" in such a crowd. We also referred such complaints back to the increasingly complex process of decision-making and choices that face us in our personal lives and our work, as well as the socio-political problems of our varied "outside worlds", that also included such an "International" association. In addition, all this was coming upon us at the start of a fresh and unknown millennium, with its own global anxiety and uncertainties.

As convenors, it was our task to hold such tensions as these and to work with them. We were also aware that English was not the mother tongue of many who attended. There was no simultaneous translation for Social Dreaming, or shared interpretations. Its "language" had to be individually understood, as with all the meanings that it provided for us. Inevitably, our dreams and the Matrix too, reflected this frustration of choice, as well as diversity of input, which it was our task, as convenors, to contain and to make sense of.

What each individual consciously expects from such a congress both allows for and confirms an emergent multiverse of meanings: the tensions of which had to be "held" within our daily meeting in ways that are typical of Social Dreaming. The same is true for the start of any new era and fresh century too: one whose future unfolding was barely imaginable. (At the end of our congress—though we were not to know it at the time—the catastrophe of Sept 11th, in New York, was only seventeen days away.)

Angry interventions about difficulty of communication had lessened, as members became more sensitive to hearing what was said, or stood up to have their say, while also speaking louder too, in order to make sure of being heard. It felt empowering, and we commented that in this way, "our" Matrix had become a symbolic tool for expressing individual determination to hear and be heard, both in the context of each day's timetable, a large and unwieldy international group, as well as life itself.

On the first day, someone dreamed of *a large male buffalo, rounding up others, while the dreamer held a baby buffalo in her arms.* There were associations to the near extinction of such creatures in North America—animals that had provided the continent's indigenous population with so much, for the various needs of their lives. It was also pointed out that because of current protection, the herds were once more on the increase: even becoming pests that needed to be controlled. Similarly to the buffalo, dreams, dreaming, and depth psychology itself were not "extinct" and could grow, as would any babe-in-arms. Perhaps it too might "outgrow" itself.

The dreams that followed contained people of many different nationalities: *Spanish, South American, Portuguese, Greek and African. There was also a plane that landed safely, though the pilot was dead.* We reflected upon this as concerning the increasing diversity of the Jungian community with its different languages, as well as widely differing socio-cultural conditions: not to mention our inner worlds and theoretical vertices too. Someone suggested that the "dead pilot", still landing us safely, might be Jung himself, his flying vehicle symbolizing the psychology that he had discovered and within whose container we were all held, despite inevitable "surface" differences of spoken language, outlook, or the sometimes conflicting interpretation of his theories. These were different airlines, perhaps.

As days went by, the shared dreams changed to provide images of walls: as containers, barriers, or a rim, as well as the image of "going to the wall", pictured as extinction by firing squad, as if expressing such dilemmas. Could our psychology, with its multitude of tongues (both outer and inner) survive in a fresh and uncertain millennium? What, in the face of such polyphony, might be its ultimate post-Jungian core and how might that evolve? These were themes demanding to be thought about by us during congress (which word means "a coming together"), but dreamed of too.

On another day, someone recounted the dream of *a panel of training analysts "laying down a rhythm" that was "bluesy".* We recognized that within a band, individual melodies and improvisations could be played, over such a "bass line", or baseline. One way in which to understand this was as a comment upon the nature and importance of the Social Dreaming with which we were engaged.

We could now see how powerfully the unconscious Matrix provided a solid backing rhythm for the more intellectual daily fare of the congress itself. The "blues" was also an expression of the unhappy and complex feelings of a downtrodden and ignored race. It was from within such states, that new ways of being might arise. Jung's discoveries were also a baseline, above which different "melodies" might be constructed; and that is how it must be.

The Matrix itself was managing the hall's acoustics better. People spoke louder, or stood up to make their contributions. We wondered aloud if, perhaps, we were increasingly attuned to subtler interventions within the polyformity of the Matrix: in Jung's theories themselves; and also, by inference, at the congress too.

Early in our time together, someone sitting close to the centre of the spiral had commented on his feeling that there was an empty space in front of him into which he might fall. This imaginary space—soon referred to with familiarity, by us all, as "the plughole"—would become an important image for us all, throughout our time together. It represented both a state of "being on the edge of things", any crossing of which might lead to fresh new experiences—exciting, depressing, or disastrous—but hitherto undreamt of. It could also be imagined as a channel for flushing away our own "dirty water". There was an understandable feeling of "holding back" and a wish not to "fall in", that we allied to the understandable fear of losing all individuality in such a populous congress, as well as within the increasing membership numbers of the I.A.A.P.

Late in the programme "upstairs", a lecturer had spoken of the paintings from Picasso's Blue Period, connecting their style to the painter's depression after the suicide of a close childhood friend and fellow artist. The speaker suggested that only by allowing himself to become depressed and in expressing this illness through the new style of such paintings as these, could Picasso "work through" his own "blues" to recover his true self once more. We now reflected that our experiences, within the Matrix, might have represented something similar. First, we had held back from dropping into "the plughole". Yet only by allowing ourselves to metaphorically "fall in" and experience, through shared dreams and associations, the clean or the filthy, animal or human, the blackness and the violence, or happiness and "the blues" as well as naturalness and perversity, could we survive and transmute such images into something creative to "take home" with us. These might sustain and lead us into our own creativeness too. We were reminded again of the "bluesy" backing rhythm that had been shared earlier.

At our final meeting there was sadness for the coming dissolution of "our Matrix" that had provided each of us with so many powerful images, whether primary or associative, as well as some unexpected experiences. It had also been soulfully enlivening, within the more intellectual experiences of Cambridge, as well as the inevitable uncertainty about the fresh millennium, "2001", that was both exciting and hopeful, as well as uncertain because unknown.

We had found comfort too in reflecting upon the city we were staying in: not only as an internationally renowned university from medieval times, but one that had also become a centre for the most modern scientific research. Cambridge was not only home to Sir Isaac Newton, with his library of books still there; but the chemical structure of DNA had been discovered in Cambridge too; while it also now possessed the large Microsoft Research Centre, looking towards a future to be discovered and unravelled.

Perhaps the same contradiction of ancient and modern, with their inevitable tensions, must also become true of analytical psychology, as we move beyond Jung's original thought, while still holding on, to his once novel insights from a century ago. Future developments beckon to us too, however, that we must also take on board.

In the centre of the spiral, there was still a sense of being pulled forward and down that was not only to an outer life, "back home"; but into our own inner worlds also. There was now, as well, the notion of our next congress, in 2004, which the association had already collectively decided to hold in Barcelona. Here our fifth official language would be spoken, thus encompassing our many South American members as well.

That other language of dreams—unconscious and universal—would also once more be talking through us, by means of a Social Dreaming Matrix that Helen Morgan and I had already been asked to provide. This official invitation felt like recognition and acknowledgement of the value of such a process, in this kind of setting.

At our last meeting, the "plughole" was experienced as closing, like a sphincter, or the narrowing of a camera's shutter that happens when the outside light is brighter. Both of these notions provided us with images of something focused as well as finished, and a time to "shut up shop" (*vide* Tatham & Morgan, 2003).

This account has described a particular use of Social Dreaming, over several days, within the context of a Matrix of a hundred or more people, with shared values, as well as conflicting needs and views. I believe that what we experienced and all that I have written reveals the ultimate value of a Social Dreaming Matrix to provide a place for the acknowledgement and expression of such differences, as well as for holding such contradictions together.

Yet it also allows for a transformation, which, if safely managed, allows individuals to leave such a meeting of minds with an enhanced awareness, both of what they hoped for, in coming; what they had actually experienced; what they would take away with them; and to what or where they might be heading. The organizing committee for the Barcelona congress, evidently felt something similar.

CHAPTER TEN

"You must not be dreaming": how social dreaming may help us wake up

Thomas A. Michael

Changing organizational behaviour is difficult regardless of the technique you employ. So much of the culture is hidden from the consciousness of its own inhabitants. We use actions to manage unpleasant experiences, and then we forget what we have done. It is as if we have had an unpleasant dream and upon waking cannot quite recall the dream. Social Dreaming appears to be a way to identify elements of experience that we have buried in our cultural assumptions, and to make these experiences available for work.

I undertook to use Social Dreaming in a consultancy at a private non-profit community mental health centre in a mostly rural county in a mid-Atlantic State in the United States. The centre provides a range of services for children and adults including outpatient and residency services for the mentally ill, homeless mentally ill, families in need of support, sexual assault victims, children and youth, and those with emergency crises need for support. The services are provided mostly for the poor and those on public assistance. The county government does not have its own facilities for such services, so that most of the work of this mental health centre is undertaken under contract to the county or the State government.

The State had proposed that health care agencies should implement total quality management. I was contacted by the assistant director, who had taken his master's degree with me. He introduced me to the director of the centre, and we developed a programme to improve cooperation and teamwork among the several members of upper management to help the organization prepare for the introduction of total quality management and with other parts of the organization to improve employee participation.

The assistant director of the centre was also the director of the department dealing with children and youth. In addition to its casework with children and youth in need of outpatient support, it had a residential programme for treatment of hard to manage youths. The residential area was located at the rear of the centre, and was a locked custodial facility with a capacity for about twenty-five individuals. This department's staff members felt isolated and alienated from the mainstream of the centre. They believed that it was because the treatment modality they used included psychoanalytic and other, complex, forms of treatment.

The department director asked me to work with them to assist them in finding ways to improve collaboration and cooperation with other parts of the centre. Their familiarity with psychodynamic processes, together with the trust that the director had in me due to our previous connection, led to our agreement to undertake a series of Social Dreaming sessions. The director was an adventurous sort of man, and the idea of Social Dreaming intrigued him. The department consisted of the director, a female assistant director, and five counsellors. The director was middle-aged, while all the others in the group were younger, in their late twenties to middle thirties. An additional part-time employee did not participate in the Social Dreaming sessions.

I began the first session by outlining the ideas behind Social Dreaming: that its purpose is to gain new information about the working of the unit, that there are no "correct" dream interpretations, that participants are free to make any associations that occur to them, that a dream can be an association or link to a previous dream, and that it is better to avoid self-censorship as far as possible. I noted that my role was to participate in any way I could by trying to be available for any thoughts, links, associations, or ideas that might help us gain meaning. I pointed out that I would be listening for common themes, and I invited them to do the same.

At the first session, Gina (I have changed the names of participants) remarked that she usually does not remember her dreams but could recall a recent dream in which *she found a $10 bill in the garbage. It was in the trash,* she said.

The director followed this dream with a report of his own dream in which *he was in a house on a hill that overlooked a valley. He looked out and noticed many "ripples" in the valley. Someone in the house said that the ripples were heat lines, but the director said, I look (at the ripples) and say, "That's water!" I ran upstairs as the water swept through the valley. Then I found myself inside in the kitchen arguing with someone about how to wash dishes.* In the dream there was the idea that *the dishes must be washed.* I had two associations to these dreams, neither of which I voiced at the time. One was that the organization with its limited resources might be overwhelmed by the flood of potential clients, and the other was that the administration of the centre needed to "clean up its act".

At this point, members of the department began to pass around a package of doughnuts, and they started to eat them. I asked them about their interest in doughnuts. Did they need to be fed? My question arose out of a partially formed thought that dream sharing was provoking anxiety, and that feeding may be a way for them to calm themselves. It had not occurred to me to connect the eating with my earlier association to the concern that the centre was plagued by lack of resources: they needed more to eat. It appears that this is an example of the need to express associations even when they are not well formed.

The director then described another dream he had two weeks before. *He was decorating a room, putting up ornate wood paneling and decoration. He was involved in the task when someone walked in and said, "The room looks good, but did you see the hallway?'* In the dream *the hallway was in disarray.* The director remarked that he did not like doughnuts. He was a large, overweight man who did not pay much attention to his personal appearance. His concern for appearance was ambiguous. He wanted the centre to be smartly organized, but did not seem to care much about how he looked.

Jan, the assistant director, made what she characterized as an interpretation. Her use of this terminology is understandable since the work of the department is informed by psychodynamic theory. What she did say shows, however, that she was able to frame her association in a way that made it available for the department to use it for Social Dreaming: she said that the director's dream was that the inside of the room was good, the outside, or hallway, decayed. She continued, "The view is not broad enough; you are concentrating on one area and refusing to look outside." It was not clear whether she meant outside of the department or outside of the centre.

Jan then recounted a dream in which she was *at a carnival, and all the members of the department were there, too. The carnival was set up as a maze.* In her dream, *Jan said she needed to go to the bathroom, and asked Nell, the part-time employee, to help her find the way, but Nell left. She also asked Marge and Gina to help find the bathroom, but they were neither helpful nor unhelpful.* At this point Gina said, "Next time I'll be there for you."

Marge remarked that it felt as if Jan needed more help. She added that a bathroom at a carnival would not be one you would want to use except in an emergency. Thus, the first session reached its time limit. As is often the case, we were not able to draw any clear conclusions. We were left to ponder and to await the next session.

The second Matrix was held two weeks later. Louis began by recounting a dream fragment in which he was playing professional baseball. He added that the dream was vague and it may have been a result of watching a TV programme about Hank Aaron (one of the greatest baseball players century).

Jan related a dream about her cousin, whom she described as a nerd with red hair and glasses. *The cousin was in college and needed a date for the prom. He looked at a calendar and decided to ask a certain girl, very pretty, old fashioned, with her hair in ringlets. "She's a Christian," said Jan in the dream, laughing. "You have to watch out for Gentiles." Her cousin asked, "What's wrong with Gentiles?" Jan replied that they were a people completely isolated, in the dark, and naive.* Then in the dream *the girl came down the stairs, looking like a character in the film* Thoroughly Modern Millie.

The director associated the dream image of an isolated naïve female Christian with Nell's role as a part-time staff member. He then presented a dream that seemed to illuminate Jan's dream. He was aware of being unable to recall much, but in the dream *someone was saying "Two, three, six," and the people in the dream put the numbers together.* He added that *the staff team appeared again to be separated, with one outside member (Nell) thought of as being ineffective. In actuality, Nell had been excluded and isolated while the rest of the group worked as pairs and trios.*

I suggested that the isolated member was part of a projective identification in which the other members of the team projected their feelings of ineffectiveness and isolation into her. Therefore, Nell identified with these group projections and acted them out.

Louis made a link by commenting that the department was isolated and chose to be isolated from the other departments of the organization. As was mentioned above, the department was physically located at the back of the centre property in a separate building, away from the other parts of the organization.

The director then asked, "So we are Nell?" Jan added that Nell did have some connection with the group because she created the departmental calendar. She also pointed out that they did give Nell jobs, but that Nell could not do them because she made them too complex. For her, nothing was simple.

The director made a link to this by noting that this department used more complex organizational behaviour techniques—psychodynamics, for instance—than other departments. Although the department had received six or seven commendations from outside evaluators, he noted that nobody in other parts of the organization mentioned these commendations or congratulated them. He added that part of this might have been because of his own behaviour: he was very much involved in the overall operation of the agency. I thought about the director's own relationship to the other members of the administration of the centre. He was eager to have it working more effectively, yet he had to be very careful not to alienate his colleagues. He was, in relation to them, as Nell was to the department. This ambiguity was known to the members of the department as well, as if they identified with the director in their feelings about where they stood in the organization.

I suggested that the problem might be about how the department had drawn boundaries between itself and the rest of the organization. I had observed that the county government had chosen to locate its welfare obligations in this private, non-profit centre rather than to set up a public agency to carry out the work. The centre had a boundary between itself and the population it serves. It is located in woods on a country road, midway between the two small cities in the county. The buildings cannot be seen from the highway, nor is access easy for the poor, who comprise the majority of the client population. There is no public transportation available, and the poor clients have difficulty arranging private transport to the centre.

I offered the hypothesis that members of other parts of the organization may have projected their own feelings of isolation into the department. It appeared that the department was mirroring this behaviour in its treatment of Nell. Furthermore, it was suggested that it might be helpful for department members to become aware of that and to develop ways to manage these projections.

The participants laughed. They remarked about the intrusiveness of one member of the administrative staff and explained that this person was one reason they were inclined to make impermeable boundaries around their department. When I asked the name of the intrusive person, they did not want to say who it was even though I was well acquainted with the centre and I knew that this intrusive person was a long-term employee who maintained a great deal of control on the centre by making it her business to know everything that was going on. It appeared that by not identifying the intrusive person the department was trying again to erect an impermeable boundary.

Jan then made the association that department members were treated as if they were naïve and they therefore enacted this, for example, by not figuring out how to use the new telephone system. It appeared that the department was being viewed in relation to the organization in the same way that the department was viewing Nell, the part-time member who had been identified with the naïve Christian girl in the dream. They were making tasks too complicated just as Nell was doing. Jan added that she would like to see the intrusive administrator spend a week in their department, the implication being that their work really is complex.

Two themes that emerged from these sessions appear significant to the work of the department. The first is the struggle to maintain a clean space in which to carry out the group's activities. The house on the hill was flooded, yet there was an argument about washing dishes. The room was decorated, yet the hallway was in disarray. There was a problem finding a decent bathroom in a maze at a carnival. Part of the struggle involved others who argued about how to clean up, or about who would or would not help with a most basic need. The concern about a clean space was indeed about the actual physical appearance of the work area, but it also expressed a concern about the relation to the community, the administration of the centre, and the problem of "cleaning up" caseloads.

In the second session, the department developed more clearly the idea that it was isolated from the other departments in the organization. In this session, staff members began to make their own associations and links. An element of the department's isolation was found to be its choice of a more complex treatment modality. One result was that others perceived this department as being unable to complete tasks (to "clean up"). So they continue to receive commendations from outside agencies, but these are apparently not noticed nor mentioned by others in the organization. In addition, they are considered naïve, unable to master simple tasks like learning to use the new telephone system. The boundary that it had erected around itself was relatively impermeable.

As has been mentioned before, the mental health centre is physically isolated, and its facilities consist of a series of buildings strung out through the property. The image of the carnival maze conveys the atmosphere of the centre. Because of a constricted budget, maintenance and upkeep of buildings and grounds are marginal. The staff of the centre work hard, but convey the sense that the public does not appreciate them. Since the clientele is mainly composed of poor people in need of public assistance, the staff struggle to avoid being identified with their clients and to maintain their self-esteem. It had been suggested that the remote location has enabled the public to put the neediest members of its community out of sight, so ironically the purpose of the centre could be summed up, "out of mind, out of sight."

Freud spoke of himself as an archaeologist searching through the past for shards of experience to gain meaning for the present. The approach of Social Dreaming is closer to the formulation of Spence in his study of the psychoanalytic process, *Narrative Truth and Historical Truth* (1982). Spence holds that the process of analysis and of dream interpretation is actually a mutual construction of a narrative by the patient and the analyst. He suggests that there is no meaning as such in nature, nor is there a narrative thread in events. Narrative and meaning are human constructions, not discoveries of a narrative inherent in the events of history. Dreaming can be seen as one of the ways we attempt to bring a sense of meaning and order to events in our lives.

By now, the department members and I had constructed a narrative that included a corporate sense of isolation; a lack of appreciation for quality work in shabby surroundings; and an attempt by members of the organization to project the more painful parts of the experience. Some results were the drawing of rigid boundaries around the department in order to protect themselves from intrusions, and their reputed inability to perform simple tasks. The laughter of the group when this observation was made, together with the fact that they were able to make links with other ideas in the dreams appears as verification that they were joining in the construction of the narrative. The events had not changed, but the narrative changed the way they looked at them.

As a result of these sessions, the department undertook to re-examine its internal and external relationships. They came to the conclusion that the department was both the object of projections from the larger organization and that members of the department were mirroring that by projecting the same feelings into the part-time member. Becoming aware of this mirroring enabled them to avoid taking personally thoughts and judgments more properly understood as unconscious needs of the organization.

After five months of working through these insights with the department the director enthusiastically reported a number of changes in the department's activities. They defined several specific actions to improve relationships with other departments in the agency. They prepared newsletter articles to interpret the work of the department to others in the agency. They developed a welcoming letter explaining their philosophy to new clients and their families outside of the agency.

They also identified points at which boundaries had been overridden by other parts of the agency and they took steps to re-establish and maintain these boundaries. In one case, this amounted to posting signs indicating that they were not to be disturbed while a counselling session was in progress.

Staff members also undertook to renegotiate interpersonal boundaries among themselves. They stopped being so ready to defer to others without protest ("to turn the other cheek"). They could see this easy acquiescence to others was also a way to erect an impermeable boundary. As long as they did not engage one another in disagreements, they maintained distance and did not work through to genuine collaboration. It was possible for them to work through Jan's dream that Marge and Gina had not helped her to find a bathroom at the carnival, and the director's dream that the staff was divided, working in two's and three's, with Nell being left out. As a department, they clarified their working boundaries with their unruly young clients. They were able to examine what it meant to say, "Then, we are Nell?"

The changes that they instituted are obvious. A consultant could have suggested them after only a few minutes of observation. Moreover, they knew, for example, that there should be a rule against intruding in a room during a counseling session. They had been erecting boundaries against intrusions, but these boundaries were not useful in supporting their work. How can we explain how members of an organization fail to apply such common sense to their activities? What is it that results in our forgetting such obvious things?

> Larry Hirschhorn has identified what he calls an anxiety chain "... when people depend on one another to do effective work, when they must collaborate, one person's anxiety may trigger an anxiety chain through which people deploy collective fantasies to deny risks" (Hirschhorn, 1988, p. 42).

Using the metaphor of the chain, we might characterize what we observed as a chain of alternation between intrusion and boundary drawing. These alternating actions could be seen as arising out of anxiety. This chain extended from the community that experienced the poor mentally ill and homeless persons as an intrusion into their ordered lives. Thus, they wanted those poor people who were "out of their minds" to be out of sight. They sent them into the woods where there were sight-line boundaries.

The centre staff, in its turn, treated the troubled youth as an intrusion and relegated them to a locked residence at the back of the property. I suspect that the unwillingness of other members of the centre staff to acknowledge the commendations given to the department of youth services was partly because they experienced commendations to this one department as implicit criticism of their activities. This could be experienced as an intrusion from outside sources.

The staff of the children and youth department enacted a boundary to keep the intrusive members of the administration at arm's length. They attempted to avoid intrusion from one another by neglecting such basic working arrangements as honest communication with one another, communication with the public and with other parts of the organization and by failing to observe good work rules. Their boundaries were in response to intrusions, and not in response to the needs of the work. The director realized that his eagerness to improve the effectiveness of the management of the centre was a potential intrusion in their affairs. The State mandate to institute total quality management in the centre was an intrusion.

My own hesitance in voicing my associations about the flooding, "cleaning up their act", and the lack of resources as a reason for eating the doughnuts may have been my own unwillingness to intrude at those points.

However, an intervention that just told them they should clean up their act would not have succeeded. It would have been one more intrusion. Consultants are constantly concerned with the "resistance" they encounter as they seek to work with client systems. Attempts at interpretation of dynamics in organizations are often met with resistance. People respond to such intrusive behaviour by erecting artificial boundaries. They concentrate on the intrusion rather than on the requirements of the work system. These boundaries can be isolation, withdrawal into the self, forgetting, retaliation, resistance. The ironic result is that after we have drawn these boundaries, we feel isolated, and we have no recollection that it is we who have set up the isolation. Then we create a narrative in which we are isolated and alone.

We usually respond to someone who makes some outlandish statement by saying, "You must be dreaming". This implies that dreaming is only an individual act. Dreams also may feel like intrusions into our lives. Perhaps this is why we so often forget our dreams, and continue to isolate ourselves. In this case, it was more a matter of "you must not be dreaming". When we engaged in Social Dreaming the department staff and the consultant were enabled to work collaboratively on a narrative and to work through these issues of intrusion and isolation without embarrassment or resistance. They were able to discern the reality of their contribution to the centre and to the community they served, and to open communication about what they could and could not do together. The dreaming helped them to wake up.

A few months after this work, the Director, Mr Bob Howard, died suddenly. He was a good man. I dedicate this chapter to his memory.

CHAPTER ELEVEN

"Don't explain, just go": the creative process and Social Dreaming, Hay-on-Wye Festival, May 2003

Ali Zarbafi, John Clare, and W. Gordon Lawrence

Introduction

In May of 2003 we placed the following edited invitation in the Hay-on-Wye Festival catalogue of events:

> The Hay-on-Wye Festival is a cultural space waiting for dreams to be dreamt . . . . People will gather together to focus on the novel, the poem, the performance. This focus will mirror the political and cultural . . . pre-occupations of the contemporary world . . . .
>
> The response of the audience develops and elaborates the creative process. This echoes the Social Dreaming Matrix where participation is a way of speaking freely and thinking out aloud . . . and create . . . the stimulus for more dreams . . . .
>
> What is dreamt during the festival will create different metaphors and fresh ideas. . . . not in order to make the language fit the world but as an invention to experience our own contingency. There is no indisputable truth to be gleaned, the thing is the experience itself.
>
> Like the matrix, the Festival is a container for reverie, just as a poem is a promise, evidence of things not seen.

The following Matrix can be seen as a creative response to this invitation, which, simply put, asks "What is creativity?" Twenty people accepted the invitation and joined the Matrix having not experienced Social Dreaming before but brought together by their interest in the creative.

The method in presenting this Matrix is one of a commentary keeping our thinking very close to the dreaming rather like a rider on a large whale going in and out of the sea. Many of the thoughts, which appear in this paper, emerged in three meetings the takers Ali, John, and Gordon had after each Matrix. These meetings were an important part of developing the thinking in the Matrix.

The dreams are the main engine of the Matrix presenting it with a deep imagination and the free associations slowly start emerging as a conscious thinking response to the dream images. As this particular Matrix progressed certain themes started emerging exploring the question but as "the invitation" put it "the thing was the experience itself". It was a deepening without ever getting to the bottom.

Keeping the question "What is creativity?" in mind each day had a particular shape elaborated by a number of key dreams some of which created the themes while others transformed the thinking in the Matrix. In day one the first dream set the scene.

Day One

Dream 1

It is night-time in the city a combination of London and old Johannesburg. An edict has gone out that nobody is to use any wheeled vehicle and this includes cars and bicycles. I am in a car with my children—four of us. People are mobbing the car. I have this feeling that I have to get somewhere else. I wind all the windows up and try and explain this. "No don't explain just go" says a voice. Lock the doors and windows. I edge through the crowd with my children. I knock down an old man but leave him carrying on slowly and forcefully through the blockage of people. I reach a shop with three children. I buy some black polystyrene sheeting which I cut with a paper cutter and use to move along the road surface smoothly and with great speed.

I wish I had bought more of these. My son says, "You did". I wake up "Oh good that was my dream". Relief.

Commentary

The edict points to the invitation where the dreamer with all her "known" potential represented by her children, is being invited to give up her "individual" mode of wheeled thinking represented by the car. She needs to give this up in order to get somewhere. It is also night-time—dream time—where there is very little light—the conscious awareness we are used to, and so more unfamiliar. The two cities represent two types of conscious thinking with London as "unrestricted" and "old Johannesburg" as very restricted: London a huge free flowing multi-cultural metropolis and old Johannesburg a symbol of apartheid where darkness and lightness were kept strictly separate and darkness is brutally undervalued. The dreamer exists in both places.

There is an anxious resistance to giving up one's individual mode of thinking and an explanation is being requested. "No don't explain just go" says a voice. A crowd or the unconscious is mobbing the car. The dreamer gets out and locks the car so keeping her normal way of thinking accessible in case she needs to come back to it. Once out, the dreamer and her children are "edging" through the unconscious.

This conscious care though is not enough to avoid knocking down an old man. Old man or "O" (Bion, 1965, p.17) represents a determined old wisdom to learn, by slowly and forcefully going through "the blockage" or density of the unconscious. "O" represents a necessary will or a required "attitude". It is the underbelly of edginess or self-consciousness.

The dreamer then finds a different mode of transport, polystyrene, or "dreaming" which is made of many (poly) things including dark material or oil and is swifter and closer to the ground. She "cuts it" in order to use it with cutting representing a creative thinking in this context. She wishes she had brought more of these dark materials with her but her son representing her instinctual side tells her she has. She just did not know it.

This instruction is continued in the next two dreams where the dreamer is *asleep on a metal girder in the middle of the road and is told "don't sleep there love, sleep on the mossy red brick wall" which is on a triangular grassy verge.*

The metal girder in this road is a window into what may be below this high "thinking" place. A girder is a place of lines like the Matrix with many spaces and possibilities in between the lines. Dreamtime is on this threshold of lines between two worlds. Maybe our creative side sleeps in the conscious world of light. The mossy red brick wall is also a place where nature—moss—and man made stone come together. Edges, verges and, where two worlds meet is being pointed to as an important place.

The third dream continues this theme of a search for creativity as the dreamer *finds herself wandering around and looking for something. Feeling a bit lost. A man's voice on a tannoy sounds cross. Get to the top and you will find him. The man's name is "Paul Teal". The dreamer is also looking for "Van Morrison's Band".*

A cross man is a man who suffers. The Cross represents biblically a very difficult place involving the ideas of sacrifice and suffering, the coexistence of spirit and matter for something higher or transcendental. It involves risk. The dreamer is also looking for Van Morrison's band—the singer. Van Morrison is not a musician one would associate with "high" places. So there is ambivalence in this "looking for". Though, curiously, the voice is both an instrument for heralding, therefore "high", as well as being very intimate, involving breathing from the gut.

The participants in the Matrix start having associations to the three dreams presented regarding the nature of restriction and the role of men and women, masculine and feminine. The associations start with, "Don't explain, go" which leads to "Hush don't explain" remembering Billy Holliday who was ruled by "male orders". There is a short thinking glimpse of how women or the feminine—nature, desire, play, imagination—allow themselves to be ruled by men or masculinity—thinking, rationality, logic. There is a glimpse of how we ensure we are not creative. The two "attitudes" involve a dichotomy, which points to a creative possibility. Billy Holliday was abused by men but was also a great singer. "Don't stop there love" points to a protective feminine voice telling "Love" to go on and be dynamic protecting the creative from being murdered by the speedy thoughts of the day world.

Two women in the Matrix remember how they as "mothers" unwittingly imprisoned their children in boarding schools and then mourned this. The Matrix is describing how the prescriptive mind can try to suppress the imagination.

Undervaluing the creative is continued in the next three dreams with first the idea of "maids colluding". Collusion means a coming together making one thing out of many—where possibilities are limited. This collusion is emphasized in these dreams with phrases like *"I am never around in these dreams"* and *"I don't have a home"* pointing to how creativity can live *"in exile"* as it has nowhere to settle but also needs to be on the move. It is very difficult to find a way of being in a moving place. The Hay festival is a transitional creative place and allowed for by culture as a moving "inner place" rather than a banished outer place. Creativity perhaps needs an inner home that is allowed to wonder.

In dream 6 the theme of collusion is introduced through *"I am about to be found out as a murderer." "There are dead bodies below the floor boards with fingers pointing through." "A missing stair." "Lots of missing parts." "How do I get to work?" "My father was to be hanged for a murder and woke up at the point of hanging."* It seems the social dreamers have "found themselves out" as murdering their creative side—the missing "I" or "mirror-stage". Many things have been missed and there is the possibility of waking up to "life" before one dies. (Lacan, 1986).

The ideas of potential, memory, and desire are then elaborated in dream 8 when the dreamer *remembering her school days, becomes aware of her potential and how she can rely on it now rather than other "authorities". "I knew Latin and maths and still remember them. There are various teachers I am no longer in awe of the way I used to be. I'm okay."* Latin and maths are deep or root languages close to the unconscious and the dream and these are joyfully still remembered like secrets hidden from view.

This dream leads to what we could call a transformational dream in dream 9 with the associations after the dream from the Matrix, which we have given in full.

Dream 9

I am on a path on a suspension bridge. I suddenly jump to a lower path on a cliff edge. I am completely unharmed. There are three horses. I ride the large then the small then the middle horse. No reigns or saddles. They are all strong deep chestnut in colour. Really beautiful.

Associations: Goldilocks: who has been riding my horse? Jump—surprise—landing without harm. Chekov had TB in the last third of his life. He was dying and decided to go to Siberia which was 600 miles away to a work camp. It was terrible and cold but he had to do it.

Take a leap—there is only one way to cross a chasm. There is another way—by bridge! (*Laughter and relief!*)

Commentary

There is a tangible relief and laughter in the room with this dream as the idea of a blind leap was turned into a conscious bridge across a chasm. Once there is a realization that one is okay—as in the last dream—then one is no longer blind and it is possible to reach a lower path on a cliff edge from a suspension bridge. A risk has been taken and there is no harm. We are no longer anxiously suspended. The dreamer is then to ride horses representing instinct and animal without reigns or saddles, i.e. no thought controls. The colour chestnut connects the chest to the nuts—a coming together of animal and breath, masculine and feminine, a sexual relief. A risk is a good thing. You can let go of who you are like the wild animals.

In the associations a participant asks "Who has been riding my horse?" but points to asking a profound question about taking responsibility for one's creative side and desires. The notion of risk and death is elaborated by another participant in the story of Chekov and the importance of living. Faced with death you have to do things. The transformational nature of this dream is about the dream image being physically "felt" by the participants through laughter and relief.

The leap into uncertainty is confirmed in the following two dreams. *An enormous antique cutting machine has been discovered. How does one use this new tool in this new space? There is a searching around for preparatory sketches "cartoons, fairies, Matisse"*. Matisse was known as a "Fauve" which means wild beast or animal. Fauves were a group of post impressionist painters who used exotic colours and challenged conventional use of colours. Is this the new space?

The "enormous" cutting machine points to something larger than the individual. In the associations one participant mentions the death of the author. Maybe "authorship" needs to be constantly challenged in order to remain creative. This is further developed in dream 11 where the two artists create something completely surprising and unusual. In the associations someone suggests we are faced with the largeness of the imagination, something deeper like the womb or a pattern—possibly the collective unconscious or wonderland. The idea of "awe" is continued in the notion of a new consciousness in a "nativity play" and a "larger than life moon" in the next dream.

In the last dream *a pregnant woman is giving birth but at the last moment loses her focus*. This shows the difficulty and resistance of being in this large space where awe and wonder challenge the individual way of thinking. In the associations a few participants muse around the relationship between thinking and creativity and dreaming and the limitations and contingency of both. How does one manage chance and accident? Someone flags up the idea of training or controlling the dream rather than just *"dreaming your dragon"* the most primitive fantasy creature. The dream points to the ambivalence and challenge of maintaining focus on the creative act which in the case of the baby is both natural but also extremely painful and fraught with some danger and risk. Another participant questions the idea of freedom and control and the nature of concern and how to be with the wild beast within where there may be a deep sense of order.

Conclusion—Matrix 1

Our hypothesis for the first day was that the dreams in responding to the question "What is creativity?" started with the theme of uncertainty and risk. There was then "an experience" of letting go which led to musings about the "unthought" possibilities in this new larger "creative space". The day ended though with the tension between freedom v control. How does the mind relate to the animal without one stopping or destroying the other? How does one discover creative freedom in a world of conformity?

The first two dreams in day two start with a great view representing the expanded mind in the Matrix from the day before as well as pointing to a new way of thinking.

Day Two

Dream 1

> *I am in a huge room with 20 foot high ceilings. There are four large windows. I am on a bed and have to get up but there is a constriction around my lower abdomen—an arm holding me down. I can see the head. He is alive—a body like artists, models, wooden ones. There is an awful repellent feeling. I am trying to prize the arm off me. I then realise I am on a film set; the man holding me down is Cary Grant.*

Dream 2

> *I am at a plant nursery—there are lots of courses going and a large turnover of plants. Lots of students. I however feel slow and unable to keep up. There is a feeling of anxiety and dread. The new plants are put in place.*

Commentary

The first dream points to a large room with four windows—a room with a view and a vision. The Matrix is faced with a larger consciousness. The dreamer in the bed has to get up but there is a constriction in the lower abdomen—the most unconscious part of the body—the gut, which echoes Van Morrison's voice. The arm belongs to a wooden model like Pinocchio, waiting to become a real boy.

In the plant nursery dream the question of how to understand the new space is being posed. Can one just be slow and wait for the imagination or does one have to be fast like the rational mind? Keeping up creates dread and anxiety. This is not a course but a journey. A new place is after all being found for the new plants or ideas, thoughts or dreams. This idea of something just growing was expressed by the dreamer in a free association where he felt relieved that the Social Dreaming Matrix was not about being saved, healed, or shown the way but just about being in the experience. This dream in many ways may be about rational society and the process of Social Dreaming and suggests a new way, which we know about but cannot find.

The idea of being in the wrong place repeats itself in the next dream where the dreamer is *sobbing. I move towards a dog or a lion sitting on rooftops saying "Hello I'm not from around here and you are not from around here either are you?"*

In dream 4 this "misplaced animal" is in the form of horses. "There is some bargaining going on around them but they are killed before they are used. What is the point of the bargaining?" A shape-shifting animal does not belong on the top of rational buildings like dreams not belonging on a rational course.

The horses are killed before they are "used" properly. The unconscious is missed. You cannot bargain with the unconscious. It will not wait and you are in danger of killing your creativity. An association we had in our de-briefing was to Max Weber who in *The Protestant Ethic and the Spirit of Capitalism* (1930) warned of the dangers of rationality and wondered who would "live" in this rational cage, becoming "specialists without spirit, sensualists without heart". This idea of the rational was also questioned by John Gray in *Straw Dogs* (2003) where he argued that the animal in us is very strong and we delude ourselves into thinking we have conquered the world and ourselves through rationality. Rationality faces the unconscious but it is a paradox because we need both.

The following dream is quoted in full with the associations as it suggests that a new mode of enquiry is being proposed following the collapsing of levels being experienced in the Matrix so far.

Dream 5

> *I am observing a 'plane crash. Two 'planes setting off. I am in a car and it feels quite realistic. There is a public meeting and an enquiry. I don't blame myself for this. The person leading the enquiry is Ronny Corbett.*

Association: Starting to grow and then crashing—comic acts—ridiculous—the Lion of Judah—Heile Selassie—a very small man—do you have to be big to be a lion?—Rastafarians—examples of

Mother Theresa—a lion heart—John Lennon—so small—5′ 6″—Van Morrisson—small and wide—reality and illusion—hanker for big volume—struggled with what he needed to say.

Commentary

There is a new idea in this dream that small people i.e. Ronnie Corbett, like the little dreams and plants in the previous dreams, are very significant and this gets elaborated in the free associations. One participant asks "Do you have to be big to be a Lion?" Maybe out of many small things other things, big and small, can emerge. The little old man in the first dream in the first matrix was big in his determination to experience the crowd of people or dreams he was forging through. In the associations there are many examples. The little people are enquiring about the collapsing of levels.

The theme of enquiry in the previous dream is represented in the next dream where a vast "suspension bridge" is now "full of police, security cables, and tapes cordoning it off" but these tapes are "head high" or too high and therefore missing the point. The police are worried "about a terrorist attack" or facing the unknown but "the children know this vast bridge as it is a very familiar place to them". Somehow the "thought police" don't know how to investigate the bridge.

The Matrix continues the enquiry in the next three dreams where *a black man is seen through a pane of glass. He talks to me and we become friendly. But the dreamer is interrupted by thought police attacking him with bullets and helicopter blades. Then there is a yearning for a house on a hill, which turns out to be disappointing.* In dream 9 the dreamer *experiences being engulfed through glass by a huge tidal wave.* Is it possible to experience the wondrous without being destroyed and suspending one's rational mind?

Dream 10 about a sobbing father who won't understand leads to a number of associations looking at the importance of horror stories, girders, suspension bridges, and the necessity of risk. A woman in her fifties in the Matrix relates the story of how she drove into a tree at 50 mph and survived and thought "Fuck I haven't lived my life yet!" The importance of edges and verges and danger in making people feel alive became very important in the associations with another woman saying she never went on "safe" adventure holidays.

What was the point? Another woman said that the media makes us frightened of taking risks. "We have been raped and not been able to be. I have to drive into a tree to be free."

Dream 11

I have been somewhere and go back to my car and cannot find it. I am sure I had left it there. I panic. It is dark and I have to get somewhere. Then I realise that I am actually driving the car doing what I want to do.

Commentary

The word car has been repeated many times in the dreams so far. It started with getting out of a car, to watching planes crashing from a car, to cartoon which is car and toon (which is a large tree of the East Indies and Australia), to looking at the cottage from a car park and then suddenly a car actually goes into a tree (cartoon!).

The meeting of levels is expressed by the "individual" meeting "nature". The car that was left in the first dream of the Matrix yesterday can now no longer be found but the dreamer now recognizes that he is in a car he had not known before. This is presumably an expanded consciousness and he is doing what he wants.

Conclusion—Matrix 2

Having taken the leap in day one, day two contemplates "the view" and the significance of glass maybe that one can "look" and "see" but not necessarily experience living until one goes into a tree or faces death. The wooden Cary Grant sees how he can become a real boy. So there is a tension between being in control or out of control. Windows, courses, and cars are all about controlling the unfamiliar. Day 2's Matrix throws up a paradox of creativity, which is that for a child for example an artistic act requires an act of ruthlessness (Winnicott, 1971. p. 131). The paradox is that there is a fine line between a ruthlessness that destroys and ruthlessness that creates. To be a great artist is not about caring about other people. It is just being who you are. The unconscious is a subversive agent whom one can get a glimpse of through the dream. It represents the animal, which is mindless and non-intellectual but is sensual, invigorating and has courage, excitement, and ultimately life in it. It has its own order.

The first four dreams of day 3 introduce the idea of colour and dress.

Day Three

Dream 1

> *I am going to a wedding and want to buy a dress in a shop in Italy. The first dress is pink and transparent with an oily look. It is too transparent I think. Last year's dress is not there. I try on a pink cheap nylon dress which is strewn with mud. This is my other option.*

Commentary

The idea of creative union of levels is introduced in the third Matrix in the form of a wedding where the dreamer is looking for a dress or an identity which has quality and design i.e. Italy. But it seems there are only two choices. The first is pink and transparent or fleshy and like the glass in the dreams the day before where things can be seen. There is also an oily look, which again like the polystyrene in the first dream of day 1 points to a basic or essential ingredient. The transparency worries the dreamer as too dangerous. The dream however points to the Matrix being in a new place as "last year's dress" is no longer available. The options are now altogether more uncomfortable unlike Italian designer wear. The second dress is also a fleshy pink nylon dress which is strewn with mud. The mud ensures that the dress remains in touch with its dirty nature. Nylon is also synthetic which points to the idea of synthesis, a material made by man out of oil and other ingredients. Both dresses may also point to a new landscape where new identities are being tried out.

The theme of change and movement is followed in dream 2 where the dreamer's father is in "grey" and cannot be seen "unless he moves". There is a "*Gothic house which is only a sketch or outline*" where the inside and outside are very different. There is a "*bloated shocking pink sponge in a white bathroom and a door which has a top that flaps*". The shocking pink bloated fish is in stark contrast to the grey that blends in if it does not move. Such contrasts in colour, levels, and sides points to an unknown space the Matrix finds itself in.

In dream 3 the theme of uncertainty is continued through the idea of teenagers who always struggle with identity but are also having to get to know their own desires. There is a marked contrast between the "comfortable outside and the narrow inside of a boarding school" i.e. from a place that requires no struggle to somewhere where one has to take notice to reach creativity. *"We seem to be tripping towards our goal."* Water, a theme in yesterday's dreams, is introduced as *a "flood beginning" and going "upwards"* again informing the higher mindful faculties like the teenager and her desires. The dreamer is looking for a dress but finds *"a cool dress that does not fit"* and like the Matrix or creativity is a *"crickly stretchy garment with an amazing collar". "I felt like a daisy."* Common daisies tend to be wild and grow naturally without having to be planted and the dreamer feels like a daisy, something which just grows. The first three dreams seem to be pointing to a very uncomfortable and unpredictable place. In the associations a participant mentions the similarity between collar and colour. This association led us to believe that ideas of colour and identity may be linked to the Fauve movement and Matisse in yesterday's dream where something new emerges and convention i.e. grey is questioned.

In dream 4 there is no colour at all but then the dreamer suddenly realizes *all her things are being taken to the dump in flat bedded parcels and I run after the truck. She is losing her "life", dreams, and colour.* In the associations a woman remembers Sartre who said "you create yourself out of nothing". Another association was that "you can dream yourself into being" and that dresses represent trying out different identities. Suddenly in dream 5 the dreamer seems more comfortable with something which was less comfortable before.

Dream 6 is a transformational dream in that something experiential happens which moves the Matrix onto a new level of consciousness and vitality.

Dream 6

An adolescent boy is sitting on a slatted bench alone. There is a booming voice—terrifying and godly—male saying to him "you are such a nuisance".

Commentary

This dream points to a potential in the idea of the teenager or the adolescent who is sitting on a "slatted" or possibly "hated" bench on his own and is seen by an authority from above as a "nuisance" though the associations see him as a "new sense" waiting to come off the bench. He is the budding plant and the future generation. The new creative possibility. There is a tangible relief amongst the participants at this "new sense" which suddenly in the next dream heralds the new senses where you can smell meadows, lavender, and flowers.

The "new senses" linked to smelling or the nose, is seen to herald a noticing of the animal, nature. In the associations someone mentions the emergence of a pink man who represents a melding of the below and the above. Cary Grant wore pink underwear. The pink man is the one who notices colour and the feminine underneath which informs the above.

The theme, of moving on and leaving behind having recognized a "new sense" are laced into dreams 8 and 9 where mothers say *"don't worry about me. . .go on without me"* or *"just go"*. There is a feeling that the past attachments need to be lost in order for new things to be discovered. To be with-out is also to be with no-thing and the gap is where creativity may lie. The goodbyes by the mothers in all three dreams are farewells, which are "good" and point to a journey and a new beginning. This is emphasized by a "a flowering head dress on a dead mother" in dream 10 representing a "flowering mind"—like the daisies. The minds in the Matrix have now become richer informed by the colour of the dreams. There is no going back to last year's dress. The goodbyes are a creative death.

In the flowering associations many issues are now discussed to do with the nature of authority or being an author. Where does it come from? Authority seems to be a mixture of masculine and feminine like the Cary Grant figure. Are men "uniform" or are they more creative in the case of the Rebecca Riots in Wales where men rode horses wearing women's dresses protesting against the tollgates? The recognition of the feminine in the masculine is a metaphor for the creative possibilities in the Matrix or the author. This theme of the feminine is continued in dream 11 where the dreamer is reassured by a woman pilot about turbulence but not convinced.

The reassurance is enough as to be convinced requires the rational mind.

The Matrix is now operating in the area of the gut and in-forming itself from this place and the mind now has to follow. In the associations the question of authority and creativity are linked to being aware of disability and mistakes and learning from them. What happens if one relies on one's nakedness as in the transparent dresses to create something new? The nose is an important and difficult sense.

This theme of risk is continued in dream 12 where the dreamer is on *a train of thought which like the Matrix jumps and flies* and the associations are *Butch Cassidy and the Sundance Kid* as well as *Thelma and Louise,* two men and two women who jumped to freedom. Also the theme of you don't have to be big to be effective or creative echoed in the figures of Ronnie Corbett or Haile Selassie is echoed in the Randy Newman song "Short people have no reason to live" but the association is "Randy New Man" which echoes the expanded consciousness in the Matrix amongst participants. The "Randy New Man" is the "New Hot Sense" coming off the slated bench and getting away from comfortable "sandwiches offered by the guard on the train" in dream 12 before the jumping and flying from convention.

Dream 13

I look around and see a dream walking down this long wide garden. At the head of the procession is Stefi Graf holding something in her hand; water, drink, food. There are a few people walking behind her. Two or three rows behind her is a man called Stephen. I am concentrating on Stefi, as this seems very important. I am distracted though by somebody running up behind me and bumping into me as if in a hurry. It is John who has also spotted the dream. I look back up the procession having been distracted and Stefi is not there. I walk down the garden to the bottom. There is little activity there. I come back up to meet John. I look across to my left as I am walking and see Stefi sitting on a long table with some girlfriends. I see Stephen on a higher level up the garden on another table with some friends. I come up to John and point them out to him. As I look at the table I notice a golden curly haired young woman sitting alone. John is looking at her and she looks up and smiles at him. I cannot make up my mind whether her smile is seductive, friendly, or polite. In any case John must be 30 years older than her—an old man in her eyes. I look at John knowingly but he is now very irritated. He tells me that these students wake him up in the morning and night by coming in and sitting in the garden and getting up to all sorts of things. Slouchers! They are his students and I realize we are at a university.

Commentary

The last dream of the Matrix is complex and interesting but points to difficulty in maintaining our creative focus. In order to remain creative you will at some point be distracted, as the dreamer is when John bumps into him. Once he is distracted he loses his focus on Stefi and then irritation enters this "university" where the dreams which were once a cohesive procession are now a group of disparate slouchers. We have to start again like a painting. The old man naturally feels impatient in his universe of rational thought waiting for the polyverse of slouching dreams to expand his consciousness again. We are always following and always too late and cannot capture the awe with our rational minds and will always be faced with this dichotomy. The young woman represents a new start. But the difference is that now the mind has glimpsed the possibilities in the feminine with a successful nose. A new adventure and new frustration is about to begin.

General conclusion

This Matrix started with an invitation about the nature of the creative. A number of thoughts slowly emerged in the three days. The dreams and associations invited the participants to take a risk and leave their individual mode of thinking. To wonder about why they had somehow colluded in killing their creativity by conforming to what was expected by the rational mind; to remember the importance of their creative rather than destructive ruthlessness; to be who they are rather than who they should be; to be open to change and not cling to a secure identity. To remember their desires and vulnerabilities with a pink passion and not remain in the grey; to trust in their nose and their Old determination and to not discard their intuition; to take risks and be open to possibilities; to listen out to the nature and wild animal in themselves which may be uncomfortable but fruitful. Ultimately the metaphor was to take the lead from our "natures" or feminine side rather than our "thoughts" or masculine side; to be open to a "moving polyverse" rather than an "academic universe".

The main point though is the "experience itself" which creates an "opening up" of the unthought and the difficult and this then becomes a fascinating journey which does not have answers but leads to a flowering of the mind that is the nature of the creative and the nature of dreaming.

CHAPTER TWELVE

The organization as a container for dreams

Alastair Bain

Introduction

I started this article with the title "The organization as a container for dreams". As I wrote it, at different times, it felt awkward and box like. I rewrote it with the aim of making it less box like. It wasn't until I finished what was to be the final draft that I realized what the underlying problem was. I was writing about one part of a two part relationship, as though it was the only part. What I was omitting was the organization being contained by dreams. With both aspects of container and contained present—the organization as container, and contained; and dreams as container and contained—there is a dynamic quality to the relationship between organization and dream, rather than the static, box like notion, the organization as a container for dreams.

This realization has led me on to thinking about dreams as mediating, or being intermediaries, between "poles". One of the poles is the Individual. The other pole is the circumstances of the Individual, which is defining identity and being, within a field at that time, for example, a book that is being written, a relationship with a psychoanalyst, or one's lover, or to God, or being at work, or living in a particular society. I suggest that there is a potential energy between these poles that occurs as a result of waking life, and that dreams balance this relationship.

Visually I see it, for example, as:

Dream
I ———————————— O
Waking Life

In this case the poles are the Individual and the Organization. There is a waking life relationship with the Organization, and a dream life relationship to the Organization, that balances the overall relationship.

There are different settings that bring dreams about particular polarities to the forefront of consciousness, and indeed probably stimulate these dreams. One of these settings is psychoanalysis, another is the Social Dreaming Matrix, as used in different social systems, e.g. organization, group relations conference, training programme, political party.

In this article I have concentrated on containers for dreaming, in particular the organization as a container for dreams. I am aware that this is the first part of the relationship between organizations and dreams. The second part—dreams as containing the organization—will be the subject of another article.

In the literature of Social Dreaming, and books cited by Social Dreaming authors, one is introduced to different dreams, and images. For example:

1. *A Storm Trooper was standing by the large, old-fashioned, blue-tiled Dutch oven that stands in the corner of our living room, where we always sit and talk in the evening. He opened the oven door and it began to talk in a harsh and penetrating voice [again the Voice, reminiscent of the one heard over the loudspeaker during the day]. It repeated every joke we had told and every word we had said against the government. I thought, "Good Lord, what's it going to tell next—all my little snide remarks about Goebbels?" But at that moment I realized that one sentence more or less would make no difference—simply everything we have ever thought or said among ourselves is known.* A dream from 1933 in Nazi Germany (Beradt, 1966, p. 45).
2. *In the next participant dream, the leader of this group is quite certain that he does not have to remember his dream because there will be minutes. Only when he wakes up does he realize that no minutes had been taken. Associating to his own dream, he wonders if, due*

to the common practice of taking minutes of meetings, the dream of socialism had been lost. A dream of a member of the Social Democratic Party in Austria in 1999 (Sievers ONE, this book).
3. The image of a white van occurred a few times in dreams from an action learning project with an organization programme of the William Alanson White Institute (Bain, 1994, p. 11).

The idea of a dream, and dream images, being located in one's mind, as "from" a certain setting, points to the significance of the "container" for the dreaming, and the dream possibly being about that container. Wilfred Bion introduced the concept of "container" and "contained" in order to explore phenomena in psychoanalysis. He later extended its use to exploring group and social behaviour (Bion, 1970). It can be used at a physical level: a plant growing in a pot, where the pot is the container, and the plant the contained. For the plant to grow properly, one needs the right sized pot. This example points to relationship as being integral to understanding container and contained, and that the relationship between container and contained is the key to growth; in the example given, to the plant's growth. In a psychoanalysis it could be patient and analyst's growth; for a group or organization. their growth in capacity.

Another aspect to the relationship between container and contained that Bion pointed to, and is implied in the notion of growth, is the dynamic nature of the relationship, such that the interaction may transform both container and contained. Bion gives examples of three kinds of relationship between container and contained: 1. commensal 2. parasitic 3. symbiotic. In describing the relationship between the mystic and the group, and the relationship of one group to another, he writes:

> . . . the commensal relationship: the two sides coexist and the existence of each can be seen to be harmless to the other. In the symbiotic relationship there is a confrontation and the result is growth-producing though that growth may not be discerned without some difficulty. In the parasitic relationship the product of the association is something that destroys both parties to the association. The realization that approximates most closely to my formulation is the group-individual setting dominated by envy (Bion, 1970, p.78).

In this paper I explore the concept of dreamer and dream. At one level there is no puzzle—dreams are dreamt by individuals (or at least dreams are reported by individuals to have been dreamt by them). Dreams are not dreamt by families, groups, organizations, and societies, but by the individuals within them. What, though, are the circumstances of the dreaming?

The concept of container and contained is useful in this exploration of the circumstances of dreamer and dream, in various ways: as an abstraction linking different system levels; providing reversible perspective (dream containing the dreamer); pointing to a relationship; and in a symbiotic relationship of dreamer and dream, pointing to growth of dreamer, or the circumstances of dreamer and dream.

The article is in two parts: first, an exploration of some of the different containers for dreaming and secondly, a short case history of organizational dreaming.

Freud, Jung, Beradt, and Lawrence

Freud wrote: "The interpretation of dreams is the royal road to a knowledge of the unconscious activities of the mind" (Freud, 1900, p. 608). But whose mind? For Freud the answer would have seemed self evident, it was the mind of the patient in psychoanalysis. Freud demonstrated that dreams have a personal meaning, and that to associate to dreams, and interpret them, could lead to insight for the patient. Freud did this through the container of psychoanalysis, a two person relationship, which can be broadly defined, as having the task of exploring what transpires in the relationship, or the mind that is generated.

The Interpretation of Dreams was published in 1900. As psychoanalysis began to grow in influence in the 20th century dreams came to be regarded in Western societies as to do with the individual, and that the dream meaning had its locus in the individual. Jung extended this vertex to the individuals' dreams also reflecting archetypal patterns present in the psyche, and that dreams were not just to do with the individual unconscious, but also a shared collective unconscious. The container for these observations, and hypotheses, was the two person relationship of analytical psychology linked to Jung's reading and understanding of mythology, religion, and spirituality. Whose mind? in relationship to the dreams of a patient, was both the mind of the individual, and the mind of connectedness as part of being human and divine.

Charlotte Beradt's investigation of the dreams of people living in Nazi Germany (Beradt, 1966) in the 1930s brought a new meaning to the question, whose mind? Between 1933 and 1939 Charlotte Beradt gathered about 300 dreams from a variety of people living in Germany. The dreams need little or no interpretation, and speak for themselves about the omnipresence of the Nazi totalitarian regime. These dreams are truly "social" dreams. In this case whose mind? is the mind of people living in Germany under the Nazi regime.

Beradt's work inspired W. Gordon Lawrence on his Social Dreaming quest, which started in 1982. Lawrence and Daniel had a double idea they wanted to explore. The first, following Beradt, was that dreams could reflect "social" realities, and the second, was that the exploration be carried out in a "Matrix". The idea of the Matrix was that it means out of which something grows (Latin for "uterus"), and that it could be distinguished from a "group", particularly the idea in people's minds of a group with a "Tavistock" meaning attached. The idea of the Matrix was partly to free people up from the restraints of being numbed by basic assumption behaviour, or being beguiled into thinking about little but basic assumption behaviour.

This venture was a success, and the evidence that emerged during Social Dreaming conferences and Matrices in Israel, United States, Australia, U.K., Germany, Sweden, India, France, Italy, and other European countries indicated the validity of the idea of the "social" content of dreams. However Social Dreaming was always a lot more than that. I was always interested in another meaning of "social", not just social in the sense of a social reality one inhabits with others that includes political, economic, moral, and other societal aspects, but also "social" in the sense of the "Matrix" itself, and the people in it. What was being grown, and illuminated, within that Matrix, and was about that Matrix, either on its own, or as a subsystem of a larger system?

The hypothesis I wish to put forward is that dreams, and their content, are a function of the container in which they are dreamt. The nature of this container, and its task, will stimulate dreams, associations, and connections which are relevant to the functioning and growth of the container. Attachment to the "individual" as the locus for meaning and as the container prevents other loci, and systems, e.g. organization, becoming the loci for meaning.

The concept of the Social Dreaming Matrix, and the practice of Social Dreaming, has been immensely helpful in freeing us from the simplistic idea that "the dream is about the individual", and in illuminating social realities (*Vide,* e.g. Biran, 1999, Sievers, 2004). At the same time, the word "social" in "social dreaming" has obscured the multitude of containers that fall within the rubric "social", and has distracted from the sensitivity of dreams, both in their generation and content, to the particular social container within which they are dreamt.

What I am suggesting is a spectrum of space/time containers for dreaming, beginning with the individual, the couple as in psychoanalysis, a family, an organization, a political party, a community, a tribe, a society, the world, and cosmos. I am also suggesting, as the title of this paper indicates, that specifying the container for the dreaming is significant i.e. organizational dreaming, as this identifies the locus for the dreaming, and for the meaning that may be sought. "Organizational dreaming" is part of Social Dreaming, but more specifically it is "Organizational Dreaming". Social Dreaming would seem to be the right words when describing a Matrix of people unconnected except through the wish to share dreams, or the dreams of a society, as Beradt collected, or when it is used generically.

An implication is that there is a "meaning vertex" for dreams which is to be found in the container for the dreaming. This is demonstrated in the following section concerning a case history of "Organizational Dreaming". The Matrix catches, like a dream catcher, the dreams that are relevant for that Matrix, but in addition the Matrix generates dreams that are relevant for the container the Matrix is expressing, in the case alluded to, the organization.

We return now to the observation of Freud: "The interpretation of dreams is the royal road to a knowledge of the unconscious activities of the mind." I suggest that the mind may be the expression of an individual, an organization, a society, and so on. So, the interpretation of dreams is the royal road to knowledge of the unconscious activities of the mind of the organization, the mind of society etc., depending on the container for the dreaming.

It might be argued that there are successively larger containers for the dreaming—individual, family, group, organization, political party, society and so on—and some of these entities are part of other entities which is true. As such how does one know what container the dream is reflecting? My answer to this is one doesn't unless the container is tacitly specified as in a psychoanalysis, a community like the Senoi, or explicitly as in the task, for example, of organizational dreaming, or political party dreaming.

The same dream may also illuminate different realities e.g. for a patient in psychoanalysis, and who is also a member of an Organizational Dreaming Matrix: the mind as generated by patient and analyst, and the mind as expressed in organizational dreaming. The vertex for generation and interpretation is different. (It makes me think of a symphony.)

The idea that organizations have an unconscious is not new, and has been a staple of socio-analytic work for many years. That the dreams of members of an organization contribute to an understanding of that organization, and its unconscious, is also not new. Lawrence has written that dreaming can illuminate the disconnected aspects in the life of an organization (Lawrence, 2003), which I agree with, as with dreams generated and having their meaning in other containers can illuminate what is disconnected in those containers. But until dreams are seen to be generated and have their meaning within this container, perhaps the idea of an organizational unconscious has lacked psychological reality for practitioners, at least for me it has. The step to recognizing the validity of organizational dreaming feels like giving organizations their unconscious back.

It may also help socio-analysts discuss the value of dreaming within a consultancy. I have often found it difficult to justify to an organizational client why we should be doing Social Dreaming. Often there is perplexity, and I think I now better understand why. What is often unspoken is why "we"—organization—should do Social Dreaming when our task is ABC. The implication has been that Social Dreaming belongs somewhere else. I can now sympathize with this view. If one talks however about "Organizational Dreaming" it fits, and makes good sense.

Within the specified task of Organizational Dreaming (see below) the host's role in the Matrix is also clearer—to make observations, and connections, which help explore and illuminate realities for *that* organization.

A case history of "Organizational Dreaming"

Between September 2002 and September 2003 a small team from the Australian Institute of Socio-Analysis (AISA) carried out a consultancy project with a large welfare organization in Victoria. The organization employs 600 Staff in Victoria and has responsibilities for housing, early education, employment, family, aged care, community, and social policy programmes. The project's aim was: to develop social entrepreneurial ways of working within [the organization]. Throughout the project we used the words "Social Dreaming" to refer to the dreaming that was done during the project, where now I would use the words "Organizational Dreaming". Social Dreaming was used as part of the initial organizational diagnosis, and later as an action learning project.

A content analysis of 127 dreams offered during the Social Dreaming Matrix indicated that in 46 dreams one or more members of the organization (or its clients), were figures in the dreams, and in 22 dreams the dreamer located the dream in a setting belonging to, or identified with, the organization.

The organizational diagnosis consisted of personal interviews, workshops, and Social Dreaming. We arranged that the Social Dreaming Matrix with two consultants would meet for eight 1.5 hour sessions at fortnightly intervals, between Wednesday, 9th October and Wednesday, 20th November, 2002. The 90 minute sessions were divided into 70 minutes Social Dreaming in a Matrix formation, followed by 20 minutes reflection on the themes that were emerging from the Matrix, sitting in a circle.

16 Staff from the organization took part with two consultants: Alastair Bain and Christopher Falkingham. The task of the Social Dreaming Matrix was "to offer dreams, make associations to the dreams, and to make connections between the dreams". At the beginning of the first session the consultants described the process of Social Dreaming, and the nature of the Matrix, and that their role was to concentrate on offering observations about possible connections between dreams, both within a session, and across sessions. We explained that we would not be offering our own dreams. Members knew that the dreaming was part of the organizational diagnosis.

The dreaming was generated, and held, within three containers:

1. The task of the matrix: To offer dreams, make associations to the dreams, and to make connections between the dreams.
2. The task of the project: To develop social entrepreneurial ways of working [within the organization].

3. The task of the organization: We discovered during the project that the organization did not have a clearly defined primary task. People in the Matrix of course knew what activities the organization carried out, and there was a vision for the organization that was well known: "An Australia free of Poverty". The implications of this vision, and the absence of a primary task, became evident in the Social Dreaming done in the second half of the project.

What I want to stress is that there were three aspects to the container for "Organizational Dreaming", and that in a consultancy project using Organizational Dreaming there will always be these three aspects:

1. Organizational Dreaming Matrix Task
2. Project Task
3. Organization's Primary Task

To my surprise from the first dream onwards the dreams were often populated by staff within the organization, and frequently the physical setting for the dream was identified as the organization.

In the first dream, the dreamer, a woman, dreamt:

I am at a conference on a tropical island off the coast of Thailand with Beth, Cathy, Tom, and others from the organization. After two days the convener decided to move the conference to another island. The trip was by boat, and there were two boats. She (dreamer) was being asked to get into one of the boats and she was refusing. In one boat were people she trusted, and in the other were people she was unsure about. The trusted people were telling her how safe it was but she was unable to get into the boat. The water was tranquil and blue.

This first dream, and associations to it, illuminated what was soon discovered to be an important organizational theme of there being "two camps" within the organization, and there being some danger associated with choosing one of the camps. As the diagnosis progressed we realized from the dreams that the nature of the two camps varied: those who followed an "instruction manual" approach to organizational life, and those who preferred "exploration"; the vantage point for viewing a reality that was available to staff of the organization but not to the executive; male/female differences among the staff.

The theme of there being "two camps" within the organization was echoed in the individual interviews, and workshops, and these diagnostic modalities illuminated other "two camp" phenomena, and splits, within the organization: around geography—Melbourne (Head Office) and the Peninsula; Head Office/The Rest; supporters and non supporters of the vision of the executive director; one's own team versus the rest of the organization; those with their "heads in the clouds" and those with "their feet on the ground".

Another theme in dreams and associations was the "old" and the "new". Was the organization an old organization of 70 years? Was it like a child, or perhaps it was in adolescence? How could people learn from the wisdom of older people in the organization? This last theme led on to a discussion of induction, and how newcomers can learn from those who have been in the organization for some years. One dream illustrated how something old and beautiful could be transformed through personal creativity into something new and beautiful. In this dream the personal creativity also transformed group dynamics of conflict over ownership into a common agreement.

Another theme concerned how a hierarchical vantage point—as seen from the CEO's perspective, or from the perspective of the Senior Management Group—may obscure an organizational reality as seen by people at the "coal face". One dream of this kind showed how hierarchy can obscure truth, and another how hierarchy can obscure beauty. Dreams on the theme of "vantage point", when discussed in the Matrix enlarged the perspective of the dreamers (staff). There was a holding on to realities that were presented in the dreams, realities, which were likely to be denied in ordinary discussion.

The same was true of the "two camps" discussion as it pertained to gender.

In one session a host observed that in the two previous sessions no dreams had been offered by men. During the next two sessions there were dreams where women were prominent and men disappeared into the background, or appeared ineffectual. There was a discussion as to whether the organization was, as one woman member put it, "dominated by females", and a clash of views developed as to whether gender was important at work. "We are all just people here" was one view.

The following week there was a dream of a man being helpful to another man, but the question remained as to whether men and women could together form a close working relationship? There were previous and subsequent dreams of men being violent. In waking reality some of the clients of the organization were violent men, and this, one would surmise, contributed to the texture of working relationships between men and women staff.

The truth of what the dreams contained allowed gender relationships between staff to be discussed and "held", rather than denied, within the Matrix. Again without the evident dream realities it is very unlikely this would have occurred in the way it did. The dreams, and discussion, offer a space which was not present before, and it is perhaps worth considering dreams as offering transitional space for discussion, finding other ways beyond denial and splitting, which are integrative and healing.

The experience of the Social Dreaming for the 16 members of the Matrix was for many transformational. It helped heal the split as played out by the "two camps" (in its various forms) within the membership of the Matrix; it provided a new language, a language of dreams, for the organization; it illuminated, and provided a container, for the discussion of hidden organizational dynamics; it promoted a "connectedness" between members of the Matrix; and it opened up a space for the unconscious of the organization—a space that could be acknowledged and valued. However, the experience elicited within the wider organization (those not involved in the Matrix) not just interest, but also envy, and ridicule, leading to moves to shut down Social Dreaming within the organization.

It is perhaps worth speculating on this attack on Social Dreaming within the organization. The uncovering, and discussion, of powerful organizational dynamics through the dreams and associations of members of the Matrix led, as has been mentioned, to a healing of splits between members, and development of a greater sense of connectedness. For members of the organization who had not taken part in the Matrix it must have appeared that something had taken place that was powerful, and mysterious. I would suggest that the understanding that members of the Matrix were felt to be working with threatened the fabric of the wider organizational life, and behaviour. This wider organizational life, and behaviour, was based on the very splits that were being uncovered, and healed, through the dreams, and associations. At an unconscious level I would suggest that the "two camps" way I [we] view the "organization is threatened by this new form of awareness". It should be attacked. And the new form of awareness is also envied. The "two camps" theme re-emerges, and is perpetuated, in a new form of "dreamers" and "not dreamers".

But the value of what had taken place was acknowledged within the Steering Group for the project, and support given to developing the Matrix as an action learning project during Phase 2.

During Phase 2 of the project the Social Dreaming Matrix continued to meet for another six sessions between 12th June and 1st August, 2003. nine members of the original Matrix left and nine new members joined (at different stages). While the dreams continued to be populated by the staff of the organization, and members found value in the organizational meanings that were explored, what became evident during an analysis of the content of the dreams, was that with one possible exception none of the 45 dreams reported were to do with clients. The clients of the organization are the homeless, the poor, the sick, refugees, indigenous people, the unemployed, children and families, and the aged.

During this second phase of the project the consultants observed that the organization did not have a primary task, and that the absence of a primary task was creating difficulties for staff in knowing whether their units "belonged" in the organization or not. The absence of a primary task also contributed to a see-saw feeling within the organization, of being at the mercy of fashion, up one day and down the next, and trying to build on shifting sands.

Instead of a primary task the organization had a vision, an "Australia free of Poverty". The consultants offered a hypothesis that the anxiety aroused by the reality of the tasks carried out by the organization—offering services for the homeless, poor, sick, refugees, indigenous people, the unemployed, children and families, and the aged—was denied and sanitized through denuding the dreamworld of this reality, and substituting a dreamworld of relationships between staff, or with the famous, and sometimes in settings cut off from the real world. We further hypothesized that an "Australia free of Poverty" was being acted out in these dreams, and that the absence of a specified primary task stimulated the formation of a "false" organizational world in the mind, which was evident in the content of these dreams.

It would be nice to report that this work resulted in the organization formulating a primary task. This did not happen as there was considerable resistance among the Senior Management Group to accepting the need for a primary task.

The case history has been offered as an example of dreaming generated within an organizational container. The different meanings that were sought and offered within the Matrix derived primarily from membership of the organization. A deepening shared awareness of organizational realities was perhaps the main benefit. A member of this organizational Dreaming Matrix who is now a member of an ongoing Social Dreaming Matrix (that meets fortnightly) has commented on how different the experiences are in both Matrices. This would seem to be a function of the dream container, and the different vertex for experience and interpretation.

Conclusion

What is being suggested in this paper is that the "contained dream" is a function of the "dreaming container", and that the vertex for the meaning of the dream is to be sought in the nature of the container. There is no such thing as a dream without a corresponding container, and without enquiring into the nature of this container, the dream meaning could be anything and everything. It follows that there is also no such thing as "The Interpretation of Dreams" where the emphasis is on the "The". There is an "Interpretation of Dreams within psychoanalysis", just as there is an "Interpretation of Dreams within such and such an 0rganization", or as Sievers has shown an "Interpretation of Dreams within a political party", or as Beradt demonstrated an "Interpretation of Dreams within a society".

As I was writing this section of the paper I was reminded of Tom Main's article (Main, 1977) about the Northfield experiments: "The Concept of the Therapeutic Community: Variations and Vicissitudes". In this article Main draws attention to different system levels: individual, family, group, hospital, and so on. He writes:

> In the hierarchy of systems each level of subsystem, systems, and higher-order systems has its own legitimacy, its own unique laws and dynamics and pathology, and its own claims on us for singular concepts designed specifically for that particular level (Main, 1977, p. 3).

Bion acted out of this understanding when he began to offer observations and hypotheses that were about "group" behaviour on his Ward at Northfield, where the "group" was understood as having its own systemic integrity. Dreams are a part of being human in the variety of systems we live in and have our imaginative being, and we need to allow them to illuminate our being in these different systems.

Notes

1 The original idea of dreams having a "containing function" for organizations, or organizations being contained by dreams, was Joshua Bain's. It took me some weeks to appreciate its value. I would like to acknowledge the great help Joshua Bain has given me in formulating ideas in this article. I would also like to acknowledge the nurturing dreaming, and discussions, with Christopher Falkingham, Peter Hetrelezis, and Joshua, at our weekly meetings, as fellow members of the Centre for Socio-Analytic Exploration. My thanks to the organization described in the case history for giving their permission to publish, and to the woman dreamer whose dream is quoted. The project work, and analysis of findings, was jointly carried out by the project team—Christopher Falkingham, Brigid Nossal, and myself—without which this article in its present form would not have been written. My thanks to Christopher Falkingham and Brigid Nossal.

2 For a discussion of how these concepts apply to organizational change projects, see Bain 1998.

3 It is perhaps difficult to think this thought after 9 years of dreams within a personal psycho-analysis, but perhaps the analysis which has allowed me to think this thought.

4 Staff who had not been in the Matrix began to share their dreams within their daily organizational life.

5 Main, T. "The Concept of the Therapeutic Community: Variations and Vicissitudes", *Group Analysis*, *10*, Suppl., 1–16, 1977.

CHAPTER THIRTEEN

Dream Reflection Group

W. Gordon Lawrence

Social Dreaming offers a method of penetrating the multi-dimensional, complexity of systems by releasing the creative potential of the role-holders in the organization, it is hypothesized. This is made possible by providing the opportunity for role-holders to temporarily "step outside" the organization of the system in their minds, to address the puzzles, or impasse, of the organization by looking at it from the dreaming perspective. The added-value of the Social Dreaming Matrix comes through the Dream Reflection Group which is the subject of this chapter.

Social Dreaming is simple to use but its results are profound. It has the following qualities:

- speed in accessing the unconscious and the subliminal thinking of the system;
- simple to learn and apply;
- surprising in its discoveries;
- self-managing for all participants;
- systems orientated

Most importantly, for the purposes of this chapter, is that it allows us to discern the emergent qualities of systems.

Emergence in systems

Emergence is the quality of decentralised thinking that every system experiences as its members take part in Social Dreaming. Alan

Turing grappled with the problem of morphogenesis which is "the capacity of all life-forms to develop even more baroque bodies out of impossibly simple beginnings" (Johnson, 2001, p. 14). The emergent, self-organizing system is a way of understanding the behaviour of ants (the architectonic example), through the development of the city, to the phenomena of mind in the context of the Internet.

It is a common fallacy to think of ant colonies being organized by the queen. Research shows that the queen is secreted in an invisible chamber excavated out of the earth, deep in the ants nest. There she is hidden by her ladies-in-waiting, away from all the other tunnels and chambers of the worker ants. This escape hatch for the queen is to protect her from any catastrophe that might befall the nest. There she gives birth to all the ants. The orders for this organization do not come from the queen, as it would do in political systems, but from all the harvester ants that protect the colony as a whole by safeguarding the queen's gene pool. This bottom-up intelligence is the hall-mark of self-organizing systems.

At the other extreme from the behaviour of ants is the stock market. The emergence of it is the outcome of the behaviour of individuals throughout the world who own shares in companies. The stock market has no leader, no pace-maker but the market as a whole decides on the value of shares, which is continually in a state of becoming, is always in the process of negotiation among the different owners of portfolios of shares. George Soros argues that reflexivity plays a key role in this negotiation. The stock market operates in the minds of stock-holders taking into account objective facts like war, famine, national debts, and other economic factors.

Reflexivity, which is the thinking activities influencing the events in which we participate and about which we think (Soros, 1998, p. 4) determines how reality is commonly interpreted. Winners in the stock market are those who think of the flaws in the argument and replace them with working hypotheses that recognize that all human constructs are potentially flawed because the flaws usually become apparent at some future date and are not present at the time the constructs were formulated.

All human systems have the property of emergence, or are in the process of becoming. Emergence is recognized through thinking and intelligence, which is first manifested through dreaming. This capacity occurs unpredictably and cannot be planned for or controlled. It is a common quality shared by all participants in a system which exists over and above the system as a transcendent feature. Emergence is present in all the rational, logically governed conversations and narratives of organizational systems as unconscious images, proto-thinking and thought. All systems conduct their affairs in the finite world, bounded by primary task, time, and territory but the sentient qualities of the minds of the role-holders have access to the infinite world through imagination and their dreams. The infinite is what is not-known, the thinking that lies beyond our immediate ken, immeasurably vast and boundless. Dreaming can give us unrivalled access to the infinite, which once experienced can be rendered as finite knowledge. The process of emergence through thinking about infinitude is the bedrock of creativity.

It exists but only fleetingly for it quickly dissipates. The understanding of emergence cannot be arrived at through rational, logical enquiry; it just exists as a property of all systems to be apprehended through intuition and imagination.

The quality of the being of a system—the nature of its culture, the efficacy of its conversational narratives that allows the system to carry out its work, indeed, the story of the reason for existence and continuance of the system—will determine the quality of the emergence of the system. The poverty of the state of being of the system will have a negative effect on the state of emergence. The greater the evidence of the emergent property of creativity of the system, the more likely it is to flourish and prosper.

The working hypothesis is that emergence is more manageable through the experience of the Social Dreaming Matrix and the Dream Reflection Group.

People who have experienced Social Dreaming have said that it:

- is a source of organizational intelligence
- is an antidote to arrogance
- is adaptive, flexible, and open
- locates the present in relation to the past and the future
- provides a space where authority is grounded in the dream and not the dreamer
- is generative of learning
- provides space and skills for reflective enquiry

- challenges existing mental modes of understanding
- builds high levels of trust and independence
- helps manage the transitions for change
- develops creative potential
- encourages lateral and divergent thinking
- is collaborative and dignified discourse
- is a mind set based on the idea of play
- is speaking about experience.

Application of Social Dreaming techniques

Its best applications are: in the ordinary life of an organization because the future issues and potential operational puzzles, or dilemmas, can be anticipated as they are brought to consciousness through Social Dreaming.

When the organization has reached an *impasse* in its collective thinking, Social Dreaming can break the "log-jam" of thinking in the organization. This is when the limits of comprehension have been reached through a failure of the taken-for-granted logic of the organization that has sustained it in the past.

The application of Social Dreaming, which is the crucible for the transformation of thinking, is supplemented by participants working in the Dream Reflection Group

Dream Reflection Group (DRG)

This synthesizes the themes of the stories of the dreams to make working hypotheses on the state of being and becoming (emergence) of the system.

The primary task of the DRG is: to make a synthesis of the state of being of the system, with its dilemmas and puzzles, using the evidence of the dreams of the Matrix to intuit the state of emergence of the system.

In the DRG there is space for amplification, which is to hold to the integrity of the dream by supplementing its meanings by reference to contemporary cultural and political events, for example, and by referring to dreams, paintings, novels, and plays to situate the dreaming in its social context.

How to participate in the dream reflection group?

First, the participants in the SDM are all convened in the DRG.

The task is explained and it is suggested that they each look at the dreaming experience by identifying:

1. The dreams
2. The themes
3. The links and connections among the dreams
4. The evidence of emergence in their systems

They are invited to divide into groups of four to work on the four facets, noted above.

Flip charts may be used, or each dream noted on a sheet of paper. Free association and amplification are used by the participants to expand the meanings of the dreams. Connections among the dreams are plotted. Evidence for emergence in the system is sought.

If the participants come from a shared system e.g. a company, the group can formulate working hypotheses on the state of being in the company and what it might become (emergence).

If, on the other hand, participants come from different systems the same process can be used, only it is about the discrete system to which the participant belongs.

Both groups share in common the society they belong to. Here, the participants can abstract from the shared dreaming to make working hypotheses on the state of society and what it is emerging towards.

CHAPTER FOURTEEN

Creative Role Synthesis

W. Gordon Lawrence

The experiences of Social Dreaming Matrices have given rise to other events which had to be invented to make use of the thinking processes that dreaming engenders. What Social Dreaming does is excite the unconscious thinking processes. At the private, individual level, the experience of Social Dreaming will result in the individual recalling dreams of his, or her, personal past. Because of the primary task of Social Dreaming, these dreams will not be used. They will be kept private appropriately, except if they illumine the system under study.

The working hypothesis was that dreams could be used to illuminate the personal complexities of carrying out a role within a system. This would be to evoke the parallel mental processes which are alongside all the rational processes necessary for executing tasks in a system. This is the stream of unconscious thinking which, metaphorically, is the "white noise" that is part of the stream of consciousness.

A model of Organizational Role Analysis which had been devised by Irving Borwick, who pioneered the method by which managers, in particular, could analyze their roles (Borwick, 1997). This intervention was part of a larger programme, Group Study and Action Programme which had been used in a large number of international corporations. When Borwick invented this in 1976, the idea of role and system was not part of the discourse of organizational thinking, as social scientists were preoccupied with the relationship between the individual and the organization. Role was the concept that identified the fact that individuals managed themselves in their systems, screening out the private factors of their individuality which were not relevant for role performance in a particular system. The role of father, or sister in the family context, for example, will mobilize different parts of the psyche depending on whether the same individual is performing a role in an organization or serving as a member of the board of governors of an educational institution.

The early conceptualizations of organization relied on changing the individual to accommodate to the system, and managers tried to assess and shape their workers' personalities accordingly. Borwick turned this on its head by saying that it was more effective to change the system than the personality. How individuals manage themselves will be determined by the nature of the system and their role relationships within it. So the idea of "management of self in role" came to be formulated (Lawrence, 1979).

The emphasis in Organizational Role Analysis is on the problems that managers experience. Role and system is the focus and not the personality of the individual. This method has been widely used since the mid-1970s and has given rise to much new thinking (Long, Newton, and Sievers, 2006). It is the best of methods for identifying and resolving operational issues in a systemic context.

Social Dreaming alerts participants to the fact that by using dreams to throw light on the parallel processes, other dimensions of roles could be illumined. There exist different methods using different rationales. A business consultant's perception of the organization will be based on its purpose, structure, processes, culture, and financial constraints. A human relations consultant will see problems based on the work environment, career possibilities, suitability for the work, relationships with colleagues, training, and education.

What participants all share in the experience of the Social Dreaming Matrix is the capacity to learn the value of free association and amplification which fosters spontaneity and the expression of uninhibited creative responses to the dream material. With the experience of the abstracting and analogizing process of free association, the boundaries around the connection sets of the brain are loosened. Thus, novel syntheses of thinking are made more possible.

Synthesis is the joining of elements of experience: it is the pattern that connects phenomena such as dreams, events, and emotions and forms them into a new whole. Synthesis, in this sense, is a precursor to action in a role. Creativity is an essential feature of synthesis and of role performance.

The following outline is given to participants

What is Creative Role Synthesis?

Creative Role Synthesis (CRS) has the primary task of, first, identifying a paradoxical challenge—or existential puzzle, or conundrum, or issue, or problem, or living doubt—of role, and, second, making a synthesis of the systemic elements involved to authorize a creative role.

This formulation is based on the idea that the individual manages herself in her role which is determined by the nature of the relationships to the system in which the role is carried out.

So, there is a triangle of:

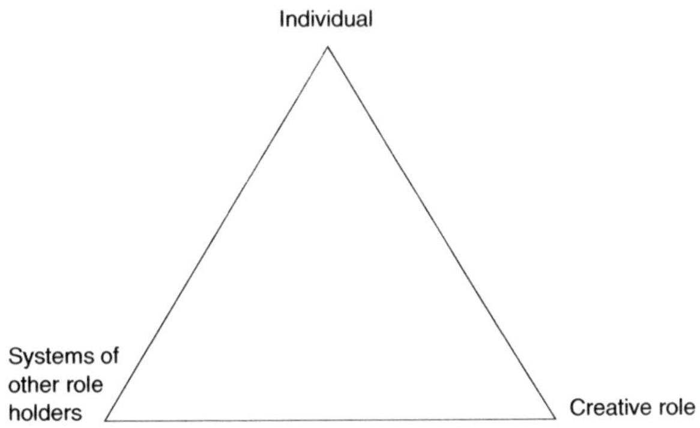

The process of Creative Role Synthesis

All participants have experienced the cultural dimensions of dreaming. After the Matrix the members will be convened in a large group. The task of the CRS will be given as well as the thinking behind it. Each participant will be given time to think of a "puzzle".

A CRS is composed of, roughly, eight members in a small group. One of the host team for the Social Dreaming Matrix will act as chairperson of the group for the first CRS. Subsequently, other members will be invited to be "host". The sequence of work has three parts:

1. Presentation of role puzzle—10 minutes [these timings can vary]
2. System synthesis—15 minutes
3. Role-System reflection—5 minutes

1. Presentation of role problem

A volunteer presents:

i. A current life puzzle, or issue, that is unresolved, in which the presenter has role responsibilities and for which creative outcomes are important to the presenter.
ii. Significant dreams they have had, which may be dreams they have had in the Social Dreaming Matrix, or which others have offered in the Matrix, or significant dreams the presenter has experienced during their life to illuminate the puzzle.
iii. Meanwhile the rest of the CRS group will take up the role of facilitator by, silently, free associating to what the presenter is saying, recalling their relevant dreams, and formulating working hypotheses on the conundrum being presented

2. System synthesis

a. After the presentation, the facilitators will be invited to speak offering hunches, feelings, and intuitions in the form of working hypotheses. They may offer their own dream to illuminate the puzzle. Free-flowing discussion is the aim. Interpretation has no place in the CRS, only working hypotheses because the system is being dealt with. The tone of the discussion is not directed at solving instrumental problems but exploring systemic dimensions of the presenter's conundrum.
b. The presenter has freedom to reply to the hypotheses, or not.

3. Role system reflection

This is an opportunity for all to manage themselves in their temporary roles in the CRS group.

a. The facilitators talk about what they have learned of the existential puzzle with their feelings and thoughts.
b. The presenter has the last word in the session by summarizing their experience of the session and what they have learned from the session.

CHAPTER FIFTEEN

The sphinx looks at the individual: Creative Role Synthesis

Franca Fubini

The infinite

Last summer I was crossing a stretch of sea at night on a sailing boat with a friend. During the long night we talked of many things and at some point I was trying to explain what Social Dreaming is. Inspired by the vast cosmos surrounding us, undisturbed by artificial light, I said that it is a bit like the starry sky above us: we, human beings, need to recognize the Big Dipper and to see the connections which create the constellations: it is necessary for shared communication and navigation.

But in the sky lit by an infinite number of stars, the possible ways of connecting them are equally infinite and we become more alive when we let some of that infinite inspire our life with a multitude of new patterns.

The infinite is one of the doors to access creative thinking, where unknown patterns and connections can be made manifest. Social Dreaming, particularly in the work of the Matrix, is a powerful way of coming into contact with the infinite.

I have experienced this over the years through a sustained practice of looking at dreams as they appear within a collective of people, by turning my focus away from the temptations of discerning individual stories and group dynamics, by keeping steadily to the task of "transforming thinking through exploring dreams by the methods of free association, amplification, and systemic thinking so as to make links, find connections, and to discover new thinking and thoughts" as stated at the beginning of every Matrix, when those words are repeated each time as a ritual for entering the uncharted space of our dreams.

My experience is that letting oneself go into that sea of connections and dreams, the excitement of truly finding a new thought which frees us, albeit momentarily from the binding of repetition compulsion is a real gift.

> Neural memory works by prototype extraction, the distillation of pure principles from the muddle of diverse experience. We have distinct linguistic labels for "memory" and "condensation", but within the brain they are one. The structure of human thought is shaped accordingly. The prototype team constitutes an Attractor—a coterie of ingrained links that can overwhelm weaker information patterns. If incoming sensory data provoke a quorum of the Attractor's units, they will trigger their team-mates, who flare to brilliant life. An Attractor can overpower other units so thoroughly that the network registers chiefly the incandescence of the Attractor, even though the fading, firefly traces of another pattern initially glimmered there. A network then registers novel sensory information as if conformed to past experience. In much the same way, our sun's blinding glare washes countless dimmer stars from the midday sky (Lewis, Amini, Lannon, 2000).

It is interesting to picture the physiology of repetition compulsion and of attachment to the known; it invites to consider how the work of the neural system and of the patterns creating memories in the brain is paradoxical: memory exists in order to help and to make life more workable (like the recognition of the Big Dipper in the sky); at the same time its selective function and bent for the known may block out any new input that is not strong enough to bypass the ingrained patterns. In this way change is missed and so is the opportunity to find a possibly more appropriate and creative response to events.

Dream-work and Social Dreaming seem to afford a means to loosen the binding of the many attractors in the brain; they provide a door into the unknown/unconscious, both social and individual, where new thoughts can grow and are waiting to be found.

However this is not always so clearly visible, and it takes time to recognize the deep work of a Matrix and to appreciate it as an end in itself. There is often a recurrent question—very relevant—at the end of a Social Dreaming experience—related to the domain of application/use in the various contexts of one's life.

Usually my tendency is to believe that we don't always need to process experiences; on the contrary, at times when the experience is bigger than our individual boundaries, it is necessary to let the experience process us in time.

But still the need to bridge a gap between the "social-istic" (in the sense of Sphinx) event and the application to one's life and professional projects exists, particularly after intense experiences like Social Dreaming conferences or Social Dreaming as a tool applied to the many levels of organizational life.

Introducing Creative Role Synthesis

How can a social-istic experience, like the one of the Matrix, reach the individual without losing the approach of a social-istic vision? Without shifting to the logic of linear thinking?

During a three day conference called "Social Dreaming and Creative Thought", held yearly in Rome and hosted by Lilia Baglioni, W. Gordon Lawrence, and myself, Lawrence introduced for the first time an event named Creative Role Synthesis, which has replaced, in the design of the conference, the Application Group—term borrowed from Group Relation—"a group concerned with reflecting on the members' experiences of the conference and making connections to roles outside the conference".

As the unconscious/infinite dream-work of sleep is mirrored in the awake and conscious space of the Matrix, so the very same process of "multiversality", and refracted thinking seems to be respected when approaching individuals' concerns in the Creative Role Synthesis.

Lawrence states that: *"a Creative Role Synthesis has the primary task of identifying a paradoxical challenge, or existential puzzle, or conundrum, or issue, or problem, or doubt of living and making a synthesis of the systemic elements involved to authorize a creative role."*

A CRS opens with one volunteer who presents his or her puzzle/challenge ("hot potato", "baggage", as defined by two of the presenters) to a small group of people who are currently part of the Social Dreaming Matrix. After a brief introduction to the puzzle, relevant dreams, either emerged in the Social Dreaming Matrix, or belonging to the past, are told as part of the presentation, that lasts ten minutes.

> A group of unknown people where I had to rebuild myself through a jigsaw puzzle of roles, emotions, dreams, and thoughts. The puzzle was already shaped by the presence of each individual, each one with experiences so distant from the one of the others and yet each one available to receive and enrich this container with the many contributions, so different and so alike (R.D., Rome, 2004).

For the next thirty-five minutes the other participants free associate, amplify the material, and offer working hypotheses, more than questions, to the presenter.

The task is not to solve "somebody else's problem" as separate to one's own, it is not to see it as something to be rid of, but through systemic thinking, that identifies common themes and patterns, contribute to the experience of creating new meaning and mental growth.

> . . . all the inputs given have become moments of reflection about myself, as though I had the opportunity to look at myself from other more external perspectives, and which have allowed me to see aspects otherwise hardly available to me (R.D., Rome, 2004).

During the last fifteen minutes a System Reflection takes place, which allows both presenter, who has the last word, and facilitators to reflect on the experience, thoughts, and feelings stimulated by the work; hopefully so to arrive at a synthesis, a space for integration of the conundrum introduced during the first ten minutes.

> There was a puzzle, now I don't know how, but the puzzle has gone (H.H. Vieussan, 2004).

A Creative Role Synthesis

A young woman consultant within a large organization, which has moved from the public to the private sector, accepts the risk of being the first presenter during the Rome conference: she feels that the structure of the event is safe enough for her to try.

> I feel it is a protected activity, based on associative chains rather than direct analysis of the events. Also the fact that there will not be questions, but only hypotheses, eases my anxiety.
>
> The puzzle cannot be thought in advance, it shapes itself during the narrative. I talk of my doubts about working within the organization and the desire to be freelance, as I was before.
>
> I talk in terms of existential values and job satisfaction, rather than logical and financial criteria . . . I need to let the group know that my priorities are linked to self realization, therefore not subjected only to the analysis of objective motivations (N.G., Rome, 2004).

The dreams

> *A friend of mine affected by leukaemia comes to visit with her German husband; I hug her, she is well now. There is a strong feeling of unforeseen wellbeing.*
>
> *Along a path in the countryside, I see my father, he his smiling. I tell him "your absence (he is dead) is not real".*
>
> *I am a small child, I wear a white dress, I put the plug into the socket and get an electric shock. It is a mute dream.*
>
> *My mother is running after me along the corridors of our home, she has a knife in her hand and wants to kill me.*

(The last two dreams are from a very early age and recurrent.)

What follows is selected from some of the material offered during the system synthesis in the process of amplification, resonance, and working hypothesis that result from the dialogue amongst facilitators and presenter.

Many angles of vision are touched, from the political aspects that regulate organizations, to the problems "linked with acquisition/ unemployment/ mobility that exist in my work context, even if I have not talked about them". This arises from an association to the dream of the couple: she has leukaemia and he is German: the marriage of an unhealthy (business) partner with a healthy/German one, living the conflict of two very separate entities. Connections expand the narrative. A link is suggested between the father and the friend affected by leukaemia. Blood, roots, belonging that can become malignant. Feelings of claustrophobia are picked up, associated with the definition that the presenter gives of her two recurrent past dreams: dreams of constriction.

The puzzle acquires different facets and associations enter into her need for a private space, the space in between: the gap. She will call it, in her further reflections, unshared with the group, the Psychoanalytical Space (the School).

Associated with the impossibility of keeping oneself on the border (free), when in fact she feels sucked into the vortex of the organization.

A dream is offered by one of the facilitators.

I am washing my genitals in the bidet, the water goes down the plug, there are eggs in the bidet.

The presenter talks of her desire to conceive and become a mother. She feels the connection with the woman who offered her dream. She associates with the title of a book mentioned earlier in the Matrix *Lovely Bones* by Alice Sebold .

The dream of the mother running after her with a knife is associated playing with the Italian word for blade "lama", "alma" (soul), "l'ama" (she/he loves her), "mala" (bad), "mare" (sea).

Interestingly enough most of those very same themes will emerge in the first dream offered at the beginning of the following Social Dreaming Matrix by another participant, just pointing to how CRS and Social Dreaming Matrix are different facets of a similar dreamwork process.

I am sitting at my desk and writing on my laptop the following words "I am about to have a nervous breakdown: technology will never have . . . a word which expresses what is between communication and translation which I cannot find. A dear friend arrives and gives me a transformer which allows the translation from the language of technology to that of the soul.

The last associations of the CRS go to rigid models, nuns, and rules; between the freedom given by a religious order and the rigidity that might imprison—a theme that will emerge also later in the course of the conference. The System Reflection is in the words of the presenter:

> Very intense, I feel that at first when I presented myself and my dreams I had put a wall between myself and the group. Slowly the participants have become closer, some more than others even if I don't remember the content of what they said. I have received a contribution to see my happiness and the possibility to see poetry where I was seeing only constraint. Now I know that I have lied: my real problem at work is not the one presented, but it has remained inside myself, even if I have treasured the whole experience . . . I look differently at my own emergencies and at my thoughts related to them.
>
> . . . it is a pity that my analyst cannot answer my dreams with his own (N.G., Rome, 2004).

When we talk about the event, weeks after the conference, she remembers it as one of the most effective experiences, where even if the distance between what she knew about her puzzle could not be filled into the participants, she got the unique opportunity to reflect on her themes, reach a new different synthesis, and find new thoughts.

Creative Role Synthesis and the Social Dreaming Matrix

CRS opens with the individual presenting his or her puzzle, however the same language of the Social Dreaming Matrix is kept: associations, amplification, resonance, finding links and connections, identifying patterns. There is no shift of methodology and the structure of the dream discourse is maintained. In fact it looks as though CRS can come to life only because, prior to that and at the source, a Social Dreaming Matrix, with its web of connected minds, is already in existence.

Both a CRS and the Social Dreaming Matrix which originates it, make mostly use of systemic thinking, which privileges common themes, links, and patterns; a methodology of thinking that comes closer to the language of the unconscious with its tendency towards one-ness and relatedness. Cooperation rather than selective differentiation becomes the currency of the discourse.

> Evolution is no longer seen as a competitive struggle for existence, but rather as a cooperative dance in which creativity and the constant emergence of novelty are the driving forces . . .
> Now, to understand the principles of ecology, we need a new way of seeing the world. We need to think in terms of relationships, connectedness, and context . . .
> In science this is known as systems thinking (F. Capra, 2002).

CRS seems to be designed so that the same language of dreams, the same appeal to connectedness, the same systemic thinking can be applied to the existential puzzle of one individual, who in a sense in the process becomes no longer just an individual, but rather the speaker for the collective, where each person can mirror oneself and resonate with the words of the presenter.

Here I would like to trace, for the purpose of explaining such affirmation, the same process of free association, resonance, amplification, and working hypothesis which is present in a Social Dreaming Matrix, in a CRS and which I mostly follow in the role of a host during a Social Dreaming Matrix. It is in a sense like tracing a pattern of thinking in becoming—I hope—starting from the small unit/cell of my thought process to the more composite one of the CRS, and to the even more complex one of the Social Dreaming Matrix: fractals and refractions, originated from the same area of mental functioning.

Social Dreaming faces life as a tragedy

Shadows

As I was collecting material and shaping ideas for this paper, two words amongst the many struck a deeper chord than the others, as though they were there to be followed, shadows hinting at something not yet emerged.

The first one in fact was "shadows", mentioned both by some presenters and by Lawrence in his first definition of CRS (shadows of the unconscious). Shadow in this case felt definitely different from the concept of the shadow in Jung, from the Freudian "shadow of the object on the ego", from Bollas' contributions; different from the use of shadow in Western art, where it is a tool for letting the light shine through (Caravaggio, Rembrandt); shadow and light, a pair of complementary opposites. Shadow felt rather as though "a something" could only manifest itself through shadows. Possible truths revealed only in the twilight or through the mist.

It brought to mind powerful images of the shadow puppet theatre in Java, *Ayang Kulit*, where, lit by candles or oil lamps (lights in movement) and behind a white cloth, the "Dalang"—a voice from the infinite—unfolds for hours in the course of one or more nights, the telling of universal truths through story; he gives voice to the many characters: heroes, gods and goddesses, tricksters and baddies, who deliver their mythological epics to the spectators.

I had the good fortune to be in Java a few times and to be part of a community of artists; there I could appreciate how art, religion, myth, and ritual are still interwoven and alive, available not just to a cultured, elite public, but to a vast majority from all conditions and status, which gathers for a performance in the palace of the kings in Yogyakharta (the ancient capital of Java) as much as they do in the courtyards of peasant villages.

The puppets are beautifully made, cut from leather, painted with extreme precision and craft, suggesting respect and preciousness. Even if in the end one can only see a shadow, still the original behind the screen is precious like the character represented.

The Dalang, an extremely respected role in Javanese traditional culture, is the bridge and the voice between the myth, the universal truths, and the spectators who are there to connect themselves with their epic roots.

So why did I think of shadow puppets in relation to CRS? Possibly because of the quality of respect and deep connection with an unfolding existential quest, maybe coated under the dress of a "work problem", or a "family problem", but which in fact mirrors for each participant the major universal themes of one's own existential puzzle.

Chorus

The word chorus evokes something closer to my culture and education, it is immediately associated with the chorus in Greek tragedy, an art form firmly connected to the same roots of human cultural heritage, which in other historical and geographical contexts have produced the shadow puppets theatre in Indonesia, the No theatre in Japan etc.

The tragedy gives voice to the myths, the archetypes of our human existence within Western culture. The material of the tragedy is always brought within an extremely powerful human content, represented with stark clarity. Representations took place during daylight and carried an extraordinary effectiveness, so that even now, 2500 years later, they can still evoke in us the strongest of the emotions.

In ancient Greece, theatre carried a purifying and cathartic value. Going to the theatre meant participation in a ritual with a social and ethical value. People were paid to go to the theatre.

Originally the chorus explained the story and the actions that the public could not see: later on the coryphaeus/speaker, became the first actor, in a representation of the relationship between the collective (chorus) and the individual (actor).

The chorus acts as a vehicle of strong emotions; it dialogues, explains, resonates with the actor and with the spectators. It becomes a bridge that articulates the choral, collective tragedy of the soul and of the human condition. It brings the voice of a collective mind.

A last consideration about the chorus, relevant to the CRS, is that nowadays the representation of the chorus is not easy from a scenic point of view: "A good chorus should be able to represent a common action, where each one is an individual, but at the same time moves in a shared ground and is in tune with the others. The worst representation of a chorus is when the coryphaeus leads and the others follow mindlessly, just an individual surrounded by sheep (from a conversation with a theatre director.)"

So what do I gather from this plunge into the archetypes of theatre?

CRS is a very novel event and more evidence needs to be gathered, but the material collected so far reminds me very strongly of and can be illuminated by images borrowed from that source.

I may even formulate the hypothesis that CRS draws its strength from sharing many traits with those archetypal models, whose language is so close to that of dreams.

A presenter stands out against the background of a collective of people. He gives voice to his personal puzzle, the others are there, not to solve, but to dialogue, to support, to give resonance to the puzzle, to mirror themselves in it, to give feedback and connections so that a new synthesis may find birth.

The process seems to give breathing space to a knot, that the more one tries to unravel by oneself through the use of analytical thinking and categories of good and bad, "I want" and "I don't want", the tighter it becomes. A collective and systemic approach eases out of the dilemma facilitating—very quickly—the entrance into a wider, dynamic, and more integrated vision.

Tragedy exists and it is essential to be aware of its existence; personal participation into the tragedy can be recognized, accepted, and made lighter.

Themes and synthesis

For more than twenty years I have heard numberless stories and dreams from my patients, each one creating a very definite and personal view of each of them. The thought that every story belongs to the shared pool of our human condition exists, but not in the foreground of my mind; when I work individually with patients it is important to tune in to each story as though it were unique.

In the course of the CRS the perspective is reversed and the themes that emerge seem to belong to the rich tapestry of human condition and cultural heritage: everyone can be touched and mirror oneself in it. They are existential puzzles revealing the tragedy of life.

The encounter with death, the injustice of it, the sacrificial victim; illnesses, the gift of returning from near death; the conflict between individual freedom and institutional demands, between private and public values; creative life versus a regimented one; life passages and the approach to spiritual contents and transformations; the suffering of unbearable loss; these are some of the themes that emerge during the CRSs.

All demonstrate a striving to find a way that goes beyond the equal pull of two different directions; in the words of one presenter:

> I am looking for a third system. I cannot see it yet, but I am moving in that direction (R.D., Rome, 2004).

Synthesis, a term borrowed from chemistry and from systemic thinking, is in fact the way in which different elements can aggregate in order to form a substance, one new and different from its original separate components.

Interdependence

Throughout these reflections the word interdependence kept appearing in the back of my mind. With this quote I would like to end.

> Consider the example of a table. The table's existence is possible due to the existence of things which we might call "the non-table world": the forest where the wood grew and was cut, the carpenter, the iron ore which become the nails and screws, and countless other things which have relation to the table, the parents, the ancestors of the carpenter, the sun, the rain which made it possible for the tree to grow. If you grasp the table's reality then you see that in the table itself are present all those things which we normally think of as non-table world.
>
> If you took away any of those non-table elements and returned to their sources—the nails back to the iron ore, the wood to the forest, the carpenter to his parents—the table would no longer exist (Thich Nhat Hanh).

They say that in Indra's sky there is a web of pearls, laid in such a way that by observing one with its reflections, all the others can be seen. In the same way each object in the world is not simply itself, but it contains every other object and in fact it is every-other-thing.

Notes

1. The existence of a multiverse is a hypothesis that the astrophysicist A. Linde developed in 1983. He affirms that what we know as our universe, is only a microscopic part of the multiverse.
2. Presenter's comments in bold.

Bibliography

Anzieu, D. (1976). *Le Groupe et l'Inconscient*. Paris: Bordas-Dunod.

Aristotle, (384–322 bc). *Poetica*. Milano: 2000.

Armstrong, D. (1998). Introduction. In: Lawrence, W.G. (ed.) *Social Dreaming @ work*. London: Karnac Books.

Armstrong, D. (1998). Thinking aloud: contributions to three dialogues. In: Lawrence W.G. (ed.), *Social Dreaming @ Work*. London: Karnac Books.

Atkins, P. (2004). Il Dito di Galileo, *Le Dieci Grandi Idee della Scienza*. Milano: Cortina Editor.

Bain, A. (1988). Social Defences against Organizational Learning. London: *Human Relations, Vol. 51, No. 3.*

Bain, A. (1994). Social dreaming and organizations: the potential. *Presentation at the AISA Seminar*, July 2. Ms.

Balamuth, R. (2003). *Childreamatrix: dreaming with preschool children—or, bootlegging dreams into the school years*. In: W.G. Lawrence (Ed.), *Experiences in Social Dreaming*. London: Karnac Books.

Barrow, J. D. (2005). *The Infinite Book*. London: Jonathen Cape.

Barba, E. (1985). *Teatro, Solitudine, Mestiere, Rivolta*. Roma: Ubulibri.

Benvenuto, B. & Kennedy, R. (1986). *The Works of Jacques Lacan*. London: Free Association.

Beradt, C. (1968). *The Third Reich of Dreams*. Chicago: Quadrangle Books. Reissued 1986, Wellingborough, Northampton: Aquarian Press.

Bion, W.R. (1963). *Elements of Psychoanalysis*. London: Heinemann.

Bion, W.R. (1965). *Transformations*. London: Karnac Books.

Bion, W.R. (1970). *Attention and Interpretation*. London: Tavistock Publications.

Bion, W.R. (1977). Addomesticare Pensieri Selvatici. *International Centennial Conference on the Work of W.R. Bion*. Turin.

Bion, W.R. (1994). *Cogitations*. London: Karnac Books.

Biran, H. (1999). *Relationship and Relatedness between the Elementary School as a System and its Violent Parts. Socio-Analysis* (2): 176–190.

Bollas, C. (1987). *The Shadow of the Object*. London: Free Association Books.

Borwick, I. (1997) *Group Study and Action Program*. New York: Borwick International.

Bowles, M. (1991). The organization shadow. *Organization Studies* 12: 387–404.

Brünner, C. (2003). *Ökonomisierung, Zentralisierung, Europäische Integration, Globalisierung—das Ende der autonomen Gemeinde*? In: Ebner, K. & Polaschek, M. F. (eds.), *40 Jahre Gemeindeautonomie*. Graz, pp. 39–54.

Cantarella, R. (ed.) (1977). *Eschilo, Sofocle, Eurpide: I TragiGreciu*. Milano: Mondadori.

Capra, F. (2002). *The Hidden Connections*. London: Harper Collins.

Coetzee, J.M. (1999). *Disgrace*. London: Secker and Warburg.

Damasio, A. (2004). *Looking for Spinoza*. London: Vintage.

Del Corno, D. (1998). *I Narcisi di Colono. Drammaturgia del Mito nella Tragedia Greca*. Milano: Cortina Editore.

Ehrenzweig, A. (1967). *The Hidden Order of Art: A Study in the Psychology of Artistic Imagination*. London: Weidenfeld and Nicolson.

Eschilo, S. (1977). *Euripide I Tragici Greci*. Milano: Mondadori.

Frankl, V. (1989). *The Social History of the Unconscious*. London: Opengate Press.

Franklin, R.W. (1998). *The Poems of Emily Dickinson*. Boston, Mass: Harvard University Press.

Freud S. (1900). *The Interpretation of Dreams*, Standard Edition, 5. (ed.) Strachey, J. London: Hogarth Press.

Gray, J. (2002). *Straw Dogs: Thoughts on Human Beings and Other Animals*. London: Granta Books.

Grotstein, J. (1997). *Bion's Transformation in O and the Concept Of the Transcendent Position*. Lecture at Bion's Century Conference, Turin.

Hack, M., Battaglia, P., & Ferreri, W. (2002). *Origine e Fine dell'Universo*. Torino: Utet.

Hahn, H. (1998). *Dreaming to Learn*. In: Lawrence W.G. (ed.) *Social Dreaming @ work*. London: Karnac Books.

Hahn, T.N. (1991). *The Miracle of Mindfulness*. London: Rider.

Hesse, H. (1975). Trans. Wright, J. *Wandering*. London: Pan Books. Orig. Publ. in German. *Wanderung*. Fisher Verlag (1920).

Hirschhorn, L. (1988). *The Workplace Within: Psychodynamics of Organizational Life*. Cambridge, Mass: The MIT Press.

Hartmann, E. (2000). *The Psychology and Physiology of Dreaming*. In: Gamwell, L. (ed.) *Dreams 1900–2000; Science, Art and the Unconscious Mind*. Ithaca: Cornell University Press.

Joyce, J. (1992). *Finnegans Wake*. Harmondsworth: Penguin.

Kaës, R. (1976). *L'Appareil Psychique Groupal. Constructions du Group*. Paris: Dunod.

Kaës, R. (2004). *La polifonia del sogno*. Roma: Borla

Krantz, J. & Maltz, M. (1997). *A framework for consulting to organizational role. Consulting Psychology Journal: Practice and Research* 49 (2): 137–158.

Lawrence, W.G. (1979). *Exploring Individual and Organizational Boundaries*. Chichester: J. Wiley.

Lawrence, W.G. (1991). *Won from the Void and Formless Infinite: Experiences of Social Dreaming*. Free Associations, 2, Part 2, No 22: pp. 259–94.

Lawrence, W.G. (ed.). (1998). *Social dreaming @ work*. London: Karnac Books.

Lawrence, W.G. (1998) *"Won from the void and formless infinite": Experiences of Social dreaming*. In: Lawrence, W.G. (ed.), *Social Dreaming @ Work*. pp. 9–41. London: Karnac Books.

Lawrence, W. G. & Armstrong, D. (1998) *Destructiveness and creativity in organizational life: Experiencing the psychotic edge*. In: Parthenope Bion Talamo. Borgogno, F. & Merciai, S.A. (eds.), *Bion's Legacy to Groups*: London: Karnac Books. pp. 53–68.

Lawrence,W.G. (2000). *Tongued With Fire*. London: Karnac Books.

Lawrence, W.G. (ed.) (2003). *Narcissism v. Socialism governing thinking in social systems*. In: Lipgar, R. & Pines, M. (eds.), *Building on Bion: Branches*. London: Jessica Kingsley Publishers.

Lawrence, W.G. (ed.) (2003). *Experiences in Social Dreaming*. London: Karnac Books.

Lawrence W.G. (2003) "The Social Dreaming Phenomenon" in *Experiences in Social Dreaming*. (ed.) Lawrence, W.G. London: Karnac Books.

Lawrence, W.G. (2004). *Flyer for The Social Dreaming Experience* hosted at the Working Men's College, London NW1, April 17th 2004.

Lawrence, W. G. (2006). *Organizational role analysis: The birth and growth of an idea*. In: Newton, J., Long, S., & Sievers, B. (eds.), Coaching in-depth: The organizational role analysis approach. London: Karnac Books.

Lewis T., Amini F., & Lannon R. (2001). *A General Theory of Love*. New York: Vintage Books.

Main T. (1977). The Concept of the Therapeutic Community: Variations and Vicissitudes, *Group Analysis, 10*, Sup., 1–16.

Mandela, N. (1995). *The Long Walk to Freedom*. London: Abacus.

Mattee-Blanco, I. (1975). *The Unconscious as Infinite Sets*. London: Duckworth.

Meyer, F. & Wiegrefe, K. (2000). *Die Schlacht der Frauen, Der Spiegel* 47, 140–146.

Moses, R. (2002). Unconscious Defense Mechanisms in the Palestinian-Israel Conflict. In: Bunzi, J. & B. Beit-Hallahmi *Psychoanalysis, Identity and Ideology*. Kluwer.

Neuhofer, Hans (n.d.). Grundsätze der Gemeindeselbstverwaltung in Österreich.

Neri, C. (1995). *Group*. London: Jessica Kingsley Publishers.

Neri, C. (2003). *Social dreaming: report on the workshops held in Mauriburg, Raissa, and Clarice Town*. In: Lawrence, W.G. (ed.) *Experiences in Social Dreaming*. London: Karnac Books.

Newton, J., Long, S. & Sievers, B. (eds.), (2006). *Coaching in depth: The organizational role analysis approach*. London: Karnac Books.

Oeser, F. (1998). *After Shakespeare—the language of social dreaming*. In: Lawrence W. G. (ed.). *Social Dreaming @ work*. London: Karnac Books.

Pines, M. (2002). Il contributo del rispecchiamento e della risonanza al dialogo psicoanalitico e gruppo analitico. In *Rivista di Psicoanalisi, XLVIII, 2*, pp. 403–411.

Roheim, G. (1934). *The Riddle of the Sphinx*. London: Hogarth Press.

Sievers, B. (1999). *Psychotic organization as a metaphoric frame for the socio-analysis of organizational and interorganizational dynamics. Administration & Society 31, 5*, pp. 588–615

Sievers, B. (2001). *Im Traum erscheint alles als normal und logisch: Die Matrix sozialer Träume*. In: Oberhoff, B. & Beumer, U. (eds.): *Theorie und Praxis psychoanalytischer Supervision*. Münster: Votum, pp. 124–142.

Sievers, B. & Beumer, U. (2006). *Organizational role analysis and consultation. The organization as inner object*. In: Newton, J., Long, S. & Sievers, B. (eds.), *Coaching in-depth: The organizational role analysis approach*. London: Karnac Books.

Sievers, B. *There is nothing more worth fighting for. Social Dreaming with the Social Democrats in Austria*. This volume.

Sozialistische Partei Österreichs (ed.), (1978). *Das neue Parteiprogramm der SPÖ*. Wien: Zentralsekretariat Sozialistische Partei Österreichs—Bundesgeschäftstelle (ed.) (1998). SPÖ—Das Grundsatzprogramm: Wien.

Spence, D. P. (1982). *Narrative Truth and Historical Truth: Meaning and Interpretation in Psychoanalysis*. New York: W. W. Norton.

Stange, P. (1994). *Silences in Solonese Dance Production. Southeast Asian Journal of Social Science*. Vol. 22.

Suharto, B. (1990). *The Concept of Mataya in Yogyakarta Dance*. Los Angeles: University of California

Symington, J. & Symington, N. (1996). *The Clinical Thinking of Wilfred Bion*. London: Routledge.

Tatham, P. (2002). *Getting to the Heart of the Matter: A Jungian Approach to Social Dreaming*. In: Chesner, A. & Hahn. H. (eds.) *Creative Advances in Groupwork*. London: Jessica Kingsley Publishers

Tatham, P. & Morgan, H. (1998). *Social Dreaming at Zürich*. In: Lawrence, W.G. (ed.) *Social Dreaming @ Work*. London: Karnac Books.

Tatham, P., & Morgan, H. (1998). *The social dreaming matrix*. In: Lawrence, W. G. (ed.). *Social Dreaming @ work*. London: Karnac Books.

Tatham P. & Morgan H. (2003). Social Dreaming at Cambridge. In: *Proceedings of the 15th International Congress for Analytical Psychology*.

Taylor, C. (1989). *Sources of the Self: the Making of Modern Identity* Cambridge: Cambridge University Press.

Thich Nhat Hanh (1991). *The Miracle of Mindfulness*. London: RiderHinshaw, R. (ed.) *Einsiedln*, Switzerland: Daimon Verlag.

Weber, Max (1930). *The Protestant Ethic and the Spirit of Capitalism*. London: Allen and Unwin.

Winnicott, D. (1971). *Playing and Reality*. London: Tavistock Publications.

INDEX